THE MARRIAGE & FAMILY BOOK

THE MARRIAGE & FAMILY BOOK

A SPIRITUAL GUIDE

EDITED BY RAVI DASS AND APARNA

SCHOCKEN BOOKS, NEW YORK

First published by Schocken Books 1978

Copyright © 1978 by Sandy Fuchs

Library of Congress Cataloging in Publication Data

Main entry under title:
The Marriage and family book.
    1. Marriage.   2. Family—Religious life.
3. Sex.   4. Marriage service.   I. Dass, Ravi.
II. Aparna.
HQ728.M285   301.42   77-87862

Manufactured in the United States of America

All photographs (but four) by Steven Noble Thomas;
those appearing on pages 51, 82, 84, and 116 are by
Raghunath Polden.

It is not for the love of a husband that a husband
is dear—but for the love of the soul in the husband
that a husband is dear.

It is not for the love of a wife that a wife is dear—
but for the love of the soul in the wife that a wife
is dear.

It is not for the love of children that children are
dear—but for the love of the soul in children that
children are dear.

Brihad-Aranyaka Upanishad

Editors' Note

We are very grateful to Sudarshan Filkow and Howard Fuchs, who spent many faithful hours at the tedious editorial work *The Marriage and Family Book* required. We also owe much to Mahesh Naud, whose enthusiasm gave the project new life at a low point, and to our editors, Patricia Woodruff and Seymour Barofsky. In all, several dozens of people contributed in some way to make this book a reality. To all these people go our profound thanks.

Ravi Dass and Aparna

Contents

Our Story

BY RAVI DASS AND APARNA

Toward the end of the 1960s, as the New Age began to dawn, we shared, with many others in the West, an awakening which filled us with a deep yearning and propelled us toward the spiritual path. Since we had no Western models that were acceptable to us at that time, we looked, among other places, to the East for forms and disciplines to follow. These we then transplanted here, some successfully, others with some misunderstanding in spite of our good intentions.

As two people who were very much a part of this new awakening in the West, even before we had met each other, we both unknowingly shared a deep interest in yoga, one of the Eastern approaches that had been transplanted here. In fact, it was this common interest in yoga that drew us together, in spite of the general conception we shared about yogis (i.e., that they were celibate, spending most of their time in isolation, meditating, etc.). To us, asceticism and spirituality were synonymous images, partly because we rejected the overwhelming material concerns of our culture, and partly because we were trapped in a fairytale notion of spirituality.

Our meeting and subsequent marriage was a significant event in our spiritual lives, one which has had many repercussions and which, in a sense, created a rebirth in spiritual understanding for us. The story of how we met is interesting to share, not only because it is an unusual story for the Western mind, but also because it describes how our mistaken views on spirituality were dissolved in spite of our resistance. The story is perhaps best told by Ravi Dass.

Before I got married I read a lot of books on spiritual subjects, but my reading was very prejudiced. I was only interested in the ''far-out'' aspects of what I read about; accounts of yogic powers and spiritual values were far more interesting to me than accounts of the mundane, day-to-day requisites for the true spiritual aspirant. I paid scant attention to ideas such as acceptance, tolerance, contentment, compassion; nor did I appreciate the foundation of all the yoga systems—the observances and restraints. I had no interest in the stages of life so eloquently described in Hinduism. I was rather like a young bull eager to show how strong I was by plowing all the fields in one day. But there were some aspects of the spiritual image I was pursuing that were very disconcerting to me.

According to the understanding I gleaned from the books I read, the life of a yogi was a life minus a mate, and certainly a life without sex. To a very ordinary, upwardly mobile, Jew-of-late-turned-seeker, this presented a tough problem but, being deep down at heart still a traditional Western achiever, I tried my level best to fit the model of what I thought a yogi was. So I was plagued by guilt, and a gnawing doubt that I wasn't really able to be a yogi. But then something happened which changed all that.

In the summer of 1971, I was living on an isolated farm on one of the Gulf Islands off the west coast of British Columbia. I had come to this farm with a close friend, AD, who had studied Ashtanga Yoga with Baba Hari Dass in India. The two of us lived in a tiny cabin and studied and practiced yoga daily. For me, life was very simple; my biggest worldly responsibility was to weed the vegetable garden and cook lunch every few days. We were almost completely isolated on this island, and we had relatively little to be concerned about.

But after about five months of this simple day-to-day existence, in spite of myself I began to wonder about the future. We were well into the fall, and it had started getting cold—thoughts of the ''world'' started creeping back into my mind. When I proposed a trip to see Baba Hari Dass, who had recently come to live in California, AD seemed quite keen too. I rationalized that it would be good to visit Babaji* to get some direction, but I was completely unprepared for the change that was to take place in my life as a result of that visit.

We arrived in Santa Cruz in the early evening, very excited and eager to see Babaji again, and he seemed just as pleased to see us; it was a very happy reunion. But almost as soon as we had settled ourselves down on his bed, he asked me, ''Have you met Aparna yet?'' After hesitating a little, my response was no, but ''Aparna'' sure sounded like the name of a girl, and I wondered what he was getting at. Babaji, unconcerned with my denial, leaned over toward AD and, in a confidential but authoritative manner, said to him, ''He knows her.'' Only a minute had elapsed since we had sat down, but already I was feeling very anxious—as if I had a thorn in my foot that I just *had* to pull out, but couldn't.

This anxiety did not let up all evening, except for very brief moments, and then Babaji's teasing would start afresh. Time quickly went by, as it does when one is really involved in something. About midnight it was time to say

---

*Baba is a term of respect often given to a saint in the Indian tradition; the suffix -*ji* added to any name connotes endearment.

good-bye and, as we were shown to the door, the girl who was taking care of Babaji smilingly handed me an address where we could stay that night. Then she slipped in, "Aparna lives there."

We drove down into Santa Cruz from the mountains, and by then even AD, usually a pretty calm yogi, was curious. He kept insisting that I must know Aparna, and I kept saying "No, I don't think so," but I was more than curious.

By the time we got to the house it was already 12:30 A.M. A light was on, so we didn't feel so bad about waking the household up. To tell the truth, I would have awakened the household even if all the lights were off.

A girl came to the door and we were told to wait for Aparna. A few minutes later, Aparna came into the room; I just stared at her blankly, as though I were in some kind of dream. Then AD blurted out, "Do you know him?" pointing to me, and Aparna responded, "No." If this seems strange now, it certainly was then. I mean, there we were—two complete strangers, confronting this girl at 12:30 in the morning! But then I lamely said, "Babaji sent us," which seemed to relieve the tension.

Ordinarily the situation could have been quite embarrassing, but AD quickly composed himself and almost immediately began pulling out his sleeping bag and preparing for bed on the living room floor. For me, the evening seemed to be just beginning. I felt a strong compulsion to get to know Aparna—I felt as if I *had* to talk to her, and fortunately she seemed agreeable. So we went into the kitchen where we sat whispering while everyone slept. We talked about everything under the sun. She told me of the summer she had just spent meditating alone in the woods of Massachusetts and how she had come out West to fulfill the desire she had had for years of meeting Babaji. We had much in common and, when we finally went to sleep at about 4:30 A.M., it seemed quite natural that we had made plans to go to Hawaii together in a few days.

We spent more than two months on the island of Hawaii, living out a fantasy both of us had had for much of our hippy years. We lived in a tent in a rain forest, ate very simple food, practiced our yoga every day, underwent an eight-day Zazen sesshin,* which I struggled through and which Aparna seemed to breeze through, and generally got to know each other a little. By the time we had decided that our adventure in Hawaii wasn't quite as glamorous as it first seemed, we had also agreed that we should marry— which, looking back on it, seems completely crazy. Because there were many times that Aparna heatedly said to me, "I have more conflicts with you than any person I've ever been with in my entire life." And for my own part, my romantic and sexual attractions to other women were still very much alive. But, somehow, both of us knew that this was it.

---

*The Zen Buddhist practice of intense meditation sessions, usually for several days at a time, broken only by regulated walking meditations and a few hours of sleep.

As soon as we got back to California, we went to see Babaji and told him that we wanted to get married shortly. But even though we were discussing our decision to get married, something was not right—Aparna and I were sitting at least four feet apart, hardly daring to look at each other, and acutely self-conscious, as if we were on stage in front of thousands of people and had forgotten our lines! This scene continued for about ten agonizing minutes, and then Babaji informed us, "I knew the two of you were to get together that night Ravi Dass came here two and a half months ago." "But how?" was our incredulous response; and with a grin from ear to ear, Babaji said, "Someone told me." We laughed—there was a lot of humor in that— but pretty soon it didn't seem quite so funny any more; I began to feel more like a dumb puppet, and Aparna became even more reserved. Babaji said to her, "Why are you so sad? You're getting married." Aparna then launched into her theories about her being more suited to a monastic lifestyle (I really began to get anxious at this point; after all, she *had* sat through eight agonizing days of Zazen without even flinching), but Babaji flashed a quick and firm "You're deluded." Phew! No place to hide.

Two days later we were married.

This was the beginning of our marriage, but in many ways it was the beginning of our spiritual understanding as well. Babaji had somehow managed to cut through many of our misconceptions about spirituality, and here we were—married! It was as though cutting through some of our misunderstandings had opened up new areas for us to grow into. So we had no choice but to let go of a lot of theories and ideas about what spirituality was and start from scratch.

The pages of *The Marriage and Family Book* represent much of the research we have done for ourselves, and many ideas and influences that we have come across since the day of our meeting, and we hope these may serve you as they continue to serve us. We now know that marriage can be a natural vehicle, a true path to God, if we only turn ourselves in the right direction with humble hearts and open minds.

All praise to the Spirit of Guidance and Oneness!

THE
MARRIAGE
& FAMILY
BOOK

I
TEACHERS AND TEACHINGS

Blessed indeed is the householder who performs his duties in the world, at the same time cherishing love for the Lotus Feet of God. He is indeed a hero.

Sri Ramakrishna

To those of us in the New Age, the truths of all the major religions, philosophies, and paths are often revealed by the teachers and teachings we are drawn to as we progress on our journey into consciousness.

Sometimes we open a book and a particular phrase strikes us, awakening us to a truth which may have been written thousands of years ago, but which now instantly catapults us into a more conscious state of being. Or perhaps we find ourselves in the presence of a great teacher, who, by the very power of his example, is able to turn us in a positive direction. But always the integration of that direction or truth into our lives becomes our work, for the path is elusive and therefore must be "grounded" and lived from moment to moment.

In few spheres is this "grounded" living of truth demanded so intensely as in the marriage relationship. Here two human beings, and later perhaps three or four as a family comes into being, are brought together by forces often too strong to comprehend, and for which we are usually ill prepared. Too frequently the "chafing" inevitable in any marriage or relationship proves to be too much, and we draw back, hide, even run away. We say we'll do better next time.

The Marriage and Family Book, however, is not a book for next times. It is dedicated to the work—sadhana—of making each moment in our marriages count, of changing what we think are curses into blessings. We have gathered a wealth of wisdom and understanding about the marriage relationship, and the real meaning of love, from the writings and sayings of several New Age teachers. These teachings are presented here in the hope that they will be a source of strength and insight in order that the reader may do the work we all must do.

We are eternally grateful for the wisdom that graces these pages, and pray for further guidance on our path.

Toward the One!

THE EASTERN POINT OF VIEW

HOUSEHOLDER YOGA
FROM THE TEACHINGS OF BABA HARI DASS

The yoga of householders is a very hard yoga.
Not for everyone.
Be householder yogis.

The yoga sadhana of householder yogis is to live
alone among people and to be in desires without
desire.

Sadhana means disciplining yourself. Anything can be sadhana—singing, dancing, painting, pottery, meditation, etc. But sadhana in a spiritual level is to attain concentration. For that too we can use any method with a thought of God.

If you can concentrate on pottery, it's good. It is your sadhana. Your aim should be concentration and method should be pottery. If aim is to make pots then the sadhana will be of gross level.

Kabir Dass was a very high saint. He was a weaver. Ravi Dass was another saint and he was a shoemaker. There were saints who were gardeners, painters, musicians, dancers.

Even household life is yoga sadhana. In household life you have to sacrifice your personal desires and try to entwine with each other. But those who think household life is just living together, for them it's no more than living together.

One can't get peace when desires are not limited. It's like a goat tied with a long rope. The goat can graze as far as she can reach, but if there is no rope, the goat can destroy the flowers, crops, or plants, or she can get lost.

This is the reason the learned people of olden times made a rope, which is household life—one-to-one relationship. A couple can fulfill their natural demands within this limit. They don't have to think about sex—because it's in hand and so it is not on the mind.

The second path, i.e., to suppress desires by force, is for sadhus or monks—those who are away from society. Their only aim is to work on themselves. They are not attached to the world.

A person can't stand in both of these boats, because their directions are different, although the end is the same.

We need three things to strenghten our sadhana: (1) faith, (2) devotion, (3) right thinking.

Right thinking is very important—a person has to find out about the traps of the world. If a person's mind is possessed with sex, for example, he should find out why and how to deal with it.

No one can attain peace if sensual desires are not kept within a limit. The family system is for limiting sensual desires. One husband and one wife and their children make up a family. If this one-to-one relationship is rejected then the mind will always search for a new relationship and this desire will never end. Some day the old body will be thrown into an old people's home, incapable of fulfilling its sensual desires, and with a mind still full of these desires. This is the greatest pain in life.

A mind full of sensual desires doesn't accept old age. This nonacceptance creates much pain in old people. They die in pain, and develop samskaras [conditioning impressions; tendencies] of pain due to not being capable of fulfilling these desires.

There is no end to desires. The more we desire, the more desire spreads roots. Contentment is the only weapon by which growing desire can be cut. In a marriage our desires need to be kept within an accepted limit by the couple. They have to sacrifice their personal desires for the union.

In marriage the problems can't be solved by divorce or separation, because the problems are in our minds and they will go with us anywhere we go. If we face the problems in one situation then our mind will learn to adjust with other people.

In some cases it becomes impossible to adjust in a marriage and in that situation divorce is important. But such cases are rare.

We are born with negative and positive qualities. No one is perfect in the world. But we can reduce negative qualities by improving positive qualities.

Acceptance, tolerance, compassion, contentment—these four qualities, if practiced in our day-to-day actions, then there is no doubt in getting peace.

It is very easy to say practice the above things but very hard to actually practice. It needs real effort, but it is not impossible to practice. One who is determined to attain peace can practice, then he or she will become aware of all the negativities in their actions.

When a man and woman are living together, whenever one gets pain and depression the other should help. It's like two people rowing the same boat. If one gets tired, the other helps out and sometimes both row together to reach the shore faster. There is a mutual understanding that they both depend on each other's energy, cooperation, and love.

from Silence Speaks (Sri Rama Foundation)

Wife and husband relationship includes all relationships. Master and servant, parent and child, teacher and student, friends, and sexual partners. If one is in pain the other at once helps by being in a position of teacher, master, parent, etc. This is the beauty of wife and husband relationship. If these relationships are lacking in any wife and husband relationship, then it's not a true marriage.

from Silence Speaks (Sri Rama Foundation)

If you have love inside, it will spread everywhere. Love can't be made and shown if there is no love inside our heart. If there is love inside us we don't need to show it. It will reflect by itself around us and will light the hearts of others.

What we have to do: not to hate anyone.

Q: What do you do about the garbage in a relationship?
B: There is no garbage, it's all manure for the tree.
The garbage comes from doubts.

Husbands and wives will quarrel sometimes because in the world nothing goes smoothly all the time. But even differences in opinion can bring you closer if you try to understand each other.

Such problems can only be solved if we solve them inside our own heads, otherwise anywhere we go the problems will go with us.

We should learn tolerance and compassion, only then can we be saved from such problems.

There is a story of a swan who had two heads. The swan would eat food with both heads much faster than the other one-headed swans. One day both heads began to argue about which one ate faster and which one ate slower. After a hot argument, they began to hate each other. One head found a poison in the food and said to the other head—I can't live with you any longer—and picked up the poison. The other head said—wait, don't eat it; if you eat it I'll also die. But the other head was so angry that he swallowed the poison anyway, and thus died the two-headed swan.

In ninety percent of householders, this kind of argument is going on and instead of compromising they separate.

from *Silence Speaks* (Sri Rama Foundation)

Tapas (austerity) for householders means limiting desires.

> Fast one day a week.
> Be silent one day a week.
> Do regular sadhana.
>
> Play, sing, and dance
> and don't fight.

Unless otherwise noted, these teachings have either been excerpted from Baba Hari Dass's letters or copied from his chalkboard.

SPIRITUAL MARRIAGE/DIVINE FRIENDSHIP
EXCERPTS FROM A LECTURE BY SWAMI KRIYANANDA

In the beginning of creation, God was without form. And when He decided to create the universe, He had to create darkness and light, positive and negative, love and hate, goodness and evil; all the dualities that we find inherent in the universe. The One Spirit had to take on an appearance, a function, of two. And so it is that we find that the basis of marriage is in infinite law.

In Hinduism, marriage is symbolized as the union of Shiva and Shakti, the Infinite and Creation. The union of the two is what this whole creation is, in a sense, really all about. We have within us, too, a wish to unite the opposites within us, to develop those things in which we may be one-sided. So it is that as people develop on a spiritual path, we find strange things happening. Men, as they evolve, become in a way feminine. And women, as they

evolve, become in a way masculine. They don't sacrifice their own character, but they become a perfect balance. You will find that, as you develop spiritually, you will begin to become, on a spiritual level, both man and woman. Not physical level, spiritual level. You will see that this is the *goal of marriage,* as it is of the spiritual path.

Men who expect their wives to be like themselves, or wives who expect their men to be just like themselves, are contributing to disharmony in marriage. I think one of the most important things for married couples is to be a little bit apart from one another sometimes, not always clinging together.

What we need ultimately is to understand that we are neither man nor woman. We are the soul. The soul has no body, the soul has no sex, the soul has no qualities, no personality; it is even formless.

I have seen very few such marriages, of such a level where there is never any fighting; always respect, always love; always a wish to grow together spiritually. Marriage should be a true and spiritual friendship, above everything else. In India they say that the best thing in marriage is for a couple to live together as man and wife, surely in the beginning, but gradually to bring their relationship to the point where they are like friends. So that their communion is on a spiritual level, and so that they are growing with one another toward God.

One of the things that one sees in this day and age, especially, I think, in this country, is fickleness. The idea that "I can give up this relationship and go on to another when things become difficult." This is very much in contrast to the traditional teachings of loyalty. In opposition to that traditional teaching, people say it is narrow-minded to believe that it is necessary to restrict oneself to one mate. But it's not narrow-minded to go deep, and you cannot go deep in any relationship unless you limit yourself to some extent.

The point is, don't be fickle in your friendships. Loyalty, my master Paramahansa Yogananda used to say, is the first law of God.

Trust, too, is one of the principles he used to hold up as important for marriage. But what kind of trust? Sometimes people trust in the wrong way. What we need to do is not trust people for people's sake, but trust them for their souls' sake. Trust them because we have given our love to this person; whatever comes from him, still I love him. *In the Indian scriptures they say that a man should not love his wife for the sake of his wife alone, but for the sake of God who is manifest as the wife. And the wife should not love the husband only for the sake of the husband, but because it is God who is manifest in the form of her husband.*

And this is how we should treat everybody.

The understanding that all is God is part of what makes possible this feeling of appreciation for everybody. If people do harm to you, well, if they do a good job of it even that can be nice. Really. When we have this feeling that it's all God, and however God wants to treat us, he probably has something to teach us, or whatever, but it's all a blessing. And if you do it that way, then you can begin to see what a wonderful show this is. It really is a lovely drama, and it needs villains, it needs comedians, it needs many things. We need to be able to step back a little bit and chuckle, and then accept.

So it is that we ought to be able to accept those with whom we live as they are, not wish that they were something else. This is a part of what they are.

We need to make our relationships, above all, a marriage relationship, a progress toward something. Toward truth, toward God. This kind of progress can come only if there is a spiritual basis.

To be able to give in, to be able to say "I'm wrong"; I think this is essential in all human relationships, but above all in a relationship of marriage. There is nothing gained to be right all the time. It is very important to be able to see where you have made a mistake, and to be able to think that you might be wrong, and then to be willing to admit it.

There should always be an effort to encourage the other partner to change and to grow. There should be a willingness to recognize change and not continue to see your partner as you have seen him or her in the past. Feed your partner positive thoughts, but then again, don't try to reform him or her. That's one of the great mistakes that you find people making. We should reform ourselves. What we should do is respect one another for what we are.

Something that Western culture has not understood is that the less a relationship is physical, the more it will be loving. People think that the more it's physical, the more it is loving. But that, actually, is a kind of self-love. It's a perfectly normal, physical human function, and it's nothing to be thought of as unclean, but we need to understand that there are higher aspects in human relationships that cannot be developed so long as there is emphasis on lower aspects. To learn to love one another in a spiritual way, to learn to love one another with consciousness, just knowing each other's thoughts and feelings, to grow close to one another in that way, this is what real love is. *And until that level of love has been discovered, you can't say that there is true love there at all.*

Everything you see in the world around you is only a mirror of yourself. And what you can understand of another person depends on what you have understood of yourself. To be able to see impartially is another matter, but where like and dislike enter into it, you are really judging, for good or for ill, your own self in that person. And when you hurt another human being, it means that you are hurting yourself. When we destroy others, we destroy ourselves; when we bless others, we bless ourselves. We have to start where we are, and grow from there. When we can accept ourselves with our faults, then only are we able to accept other people. And if we cannot accept other people, it means that, in one way or another, we have not truly accepted ourselves.

Thus, it is necessary in this divine plan for people not just to go off into seclusion and spend their time seeking God unless they have become sufficiently advanced to be able to do so without creating fences around themselves. It is necessary to live in community. It is necessary to live with other people. It is necessary because, without these objectifications of ourselves, these mirrors of ourselves, we don't really grow. We never get a chance to see ourselves clearly. What you put out may not be received, but the important thing is that you put it out in the way that will be an expansion of your consciousness and a blessing on the other person.

To love all is to turn everything into that kind of positive which is between the opposites of positive and negative in a worldly sense. It is that middle point, that center between these two opposites that we need to find; but having found that center, we come to the Divine positive, which is something which becomes less and less affected by the opposites of duality, and more and more joyous, more and more loving, more and more a flow that accepts, that embraces, that recognizes all people as one's friends.

There are many human relationships in this world, but all of them, if they are really valid—which is to say, if they are based in the kind of consciousness that will expand and uplift—really may be said to have friendship at their core. The love of a mother for her child is really the love of a friend. It has to be based in that kind of respect, all of those basic attitudes that are to be found in friendship. This is the kind of attitude that a person has when he has no likes or dislikes, when he is not attached. It's true, he can see, that this thing isn't right or this thing is right and that thing is right, but he is not affected by it. Inwardly, he is not touched. He says "Let it be." Such a person is a friend to people. When people come and say "Please help me in this, I am such and such a type of person," he doesn't sit back and say "Oh, you are, are you?" Without judging, he offers help. He doesn't try to tell people how they ought to be; he gives them the chance to grow at their own rate. He doesn't impose his values; he tries to help others to come up gradually, at their own speed and in their own life to the highest value of all, which is love for God. This is, indeed, a true friend.

It is necessary for people to have a few whom they do call their friends, with whom they live up to that ideal of friendship in the highest and the purest way. Because when they can understand what friendship is in that sense, then can they begin to let it overflow with all people in a more general way, and make that general feeling a true and genuine thing.

What we want to do is to develop a specific inclusiveness in order to develop a general inclusiveness that will be really sincere. Then when people treat you in ways that you might not have liked before, it no longer touches you. True understanding must grow from the specific to the general.

To go into relationships, particularly marriage, will evoke the highest from you. This will mean tests, difficulties, misunderstandings, all the things that happen between people, but you have to rise above to the point where you are always coming out on top of your reactions and always being more and more an expression of God to them. In no other relationship is there such complete freedom as there is in friendship, and such a relationship between a man and woman is a spiritual marriage, a divine friendship.

A HINDU PERSPECTIVE
EXCERPT FROM AN INTERVIEW WITH
PANDIT GIAN CHANDRA SHASTRI

P: The joint family system is an old system in India. We believe in this system and it keeps us happy, warm, and pleasant. In the Western world a family means wife, husband, and children, but in our system it means full unit.

God created man with one tiny mouth, two strong hands, and a strong will to work and earn. One man earns not only to support himself but to support many. We believe that a family should be together, and in a family all the people, including disabled parents, should live together. Moreover, if there are two married brothers who live together it makes a beautiful family. It is an economical way to live. Sometimes if I live alone I may feel bored. I may try to find some friends to stay with me. If I get my own blood relations to live with me it is more reliable and dependable, more trustworthy and pleasant, as it is better to live with one large family.

So if I wish to get someone to live with me, I must provide something for that. If my sister gets married, I help her at the time of the wedding. With this assurance, after marriage we will be the same as before. I assure her I will look after her even though her husband is responsible for the household; still I contribute something to help them. That really keeps us together; this is the reason that I never feel bored or alone in my mind. It keeps me busy and concerned with all, which makes me happy, and to be happy is the goal of man. So, to be economical and to be interested in man and to belong to others is the way of happiness.

The old ones living in a home help the young ones to grow up; they don't need babysitting. Grandparents have deep affection for their grandchildren and, being experienced, they can please the kids in a proper way.

In the joint family system there are problems too. Sometimes the family is poor but the members help each other. Every problem has its good points too.

RD: Old people are neglected very much here in the West. Young people put old people in old-age homes. In the Indian system they get shelter and security.

P: In this system the unabled, or disabled, are accommodated. They are supported by being in the family. If they were sent to some lonely place they would feel left out and discouraged; they would be unhappy and complaining all the time. In a family system, they have useful things to do, they look after cattle, gardens, house, children. Everyone has a place in a home—nobody is useless, and it helps those people in the name of humanity, brotherhood, relationship. This is how to keep people happy. Old people in separate houses feel quite depressed. Living in the family house they feel useful—helping, looking after, caring for the young ones.

ONE SOUL IN TWO BODIES

Two people are brought together by the unseen hand of God. Whom God unites, let no earthly power disunite. You are one soul in two bodies. Be like one candle light; be the same light in two forms. If one is asked a question, both should give the same answer. This can be done by those hearts who are together.

This beautiful union on the physical plane is, as yet, only a glimpse of the higher union, the everlasting marriage between the soul and God.

In the course of the householder's life, one does make mistakes. What should we do when we make a mistake? We should better organize our householder's life. Guru Amar Das gave his daughter three principles for her conduct in life:

"If you make a mistake, confess it; a dispute only arises if we proudly toss our heads."

"After a mistake has been made, whatever instructions are given, they should be followed."

"Abide by the will of God in pain and pleasure."

If we follow those three principles, all of the worldly duties are fulfilled.

Have a sweet tongue to speak softly and kindly. The husband will be

pleased and will act according to the wife's wishes. A tongue filled with humility is the essence of all attributes.

God has united us in marriage, and He is the only One who can dissolve the marriage.

from a discourse by Kirpal Singh

The Blessed One (Buddha) was pleased to see so many guests full of good cheer and he quickened them and gladdened them with words of truth, proclaiming the bliss of righteousness:

"The greatest happiness which a mortal man can imagine is the bond of marriage that ties together two loving hearts. But there is a greater happiness still: it is the embrace of truth. Death will separate husband and wife, but death will never affect him who has espoused the truth.

15

"Therefore be married unto the truth and live with the truth in holy wedlock. The husband who loves his wife and desires for a union that shall be everlasting must be faithful to her so as to be like truth itself, and she will rely upon him and revere him and minister unto him. And the wife who loves her husband and desires a union that shall be everlasting must be faithful to him so as to be like truth itself; and he will place his trust in her, he will provide for her. Verily, I say unto you, their children will become like unto their parents and will bear witness to their happiness.

"Let no man be single, let every one be wedded in holy love to the truth. And when Mara, the destroyer, comes to separate the visible form of your being, you will continue to live in the truth, and you will partake of the life everlasting, for the truth is immortal."

from "The Marriage Feast in Jambunada," a Buddhist parable

THE WESTERN POINT OF VIEW

Do not let the things that seem to be so important at times stand in the way of harmony. Be willing to give in. Do not always try to have your own way; and do not allow yourself to take offense to his harsh words or to threats. Try to love and be patient, but realize that you have your challenge in a karmic problem, in this, from the incarnation mentioned before, even as he has his.

Sister, you do not understand, as yet, the holiness of marriage, because you have not had the opportunity to see it and view it in the home environ in which you have been raised. There is a sacredness between helpmeet and helpmate that is not unrelated to the search of the individual for God. The kind of sexual freedom in which the one of whom you ask believes, and many of those with whom he has been associated believe, is not freedom at all, but slavery. There is no greater slave than the person who is caught up in the desires of the sexual urges and identity; and even more so to one who does not recognize the desire as being that, and rationalizes it as other things.

Also, your intellectual potentials in this lifetime should be channeled creatively and meaningfully, instead of being suppressed by the influences of the dissipation of bodily energies in sexual drives and activities; for we see that you are one who, without a personal sense of control and achievement, will find discontent, disgust, and will be inclined to blame another.

Ray Stanford, *Speak, Shining Stranger* (published by
the Association for the Understanding of Man)

To help each of you to learn your lessons . . .

The principal reason for the one coming to you as husband or wife in this life is to help each of you to learn your lessons, which evidently you have failed to learn in the past, and this time to strive more determinedly to

conquer those qualities or weaknesses in you which the other seems uncannily able to bring to the surface—each thus under the direction of the higher self actually teaching the other.

Of course, if you are still quite selfish and headstrong, and refuse to face yourself and see only those qualities in the other which show up your own weaknesses so glaringly, and you rebel against it all and seek to remain apart from the other, it only postpones the happiness and peace your human mind seeks and which your soul longs for and keeps urging you toward.

On the other hand, where human love is still very strong—and selfish, and unwilling to allow the other the freedom of life and thought which you insist upon having for yourself, and you try to force that other to think and see as you love to do—you will have to learn through much suffering and unhappiness that the strongest demand of the soul is for perfect freedom, and that one who would bind another soul can expect not love, but rebellion, deceit, and constant antagonism, if not smothered hatred.

This, however, hardly applies to one on the path. Such a one gets inner glimpses of the caged soul of the other, and strives hard to conquer those old claims of the selfish personality and even to help the other to awaken to that which is holding him or her back from what the soul is seeking. For such human love is gradually lifted up into divine love, and while the other, if anything, is more greatly loved than ever, despite all weaknesses, yet it is with a love that unites with that of the higher self of the other, as it were, in a great yearning to bring the other consciously into a true understanding of the purpose of their coming together and consequently into the same joy of the Lord that the knowing one feels.

The Living Christ Movement

THE MAYPOLE
A STORY BY RESHAD FIELD

Once upon a time, two people chose to be together.

Two rocks stood on a great golden beach. Relationships to other rocks had chipped away some of their rough edges, but the other rocks had been carried away in time by the tides. The wind blew, the storms came, and the waves thundered up the beach, and wherever there was a weakness or a crack the rock began to fall apart. After an eon of time there were no longer the two rocks, for they had both become one with the golden beach, which stretched out into the setting sun.

But, these two people knew there was another way to be together. They had heard that the time was coming for the fulfillment of the great alchemical marriage of heaven and earth, perhaps for the first time, and they searched high and low for someone who knew and understood the secrets of life— someone who would marry them.

Their search took them to a wise man whom they had heard was living in one of the tiny villages in the heart of England, where traditions are pre-served and the old way of life still thrives. Nothing much had changed, and they kept a great maypole in the town square for the yearly celebration of the dance of the multicolored ribbons, which had been handed down from gen-eration to generation from the beginning of time. The old man of the village was highly revered for it was said that he held the secrets of long life. No one really knew how old he was, not even the oldest of the ladies who sat on the verandas in the morning with their knitting.

The couple who had chosen to be together came hand in hand to meet the old man of the village and found him sitting by the huge fireplace in the back of his cottage. The smell of fresh bread came from the sixteenth-century baking oven, and hams were being smoked over the fire of oaken logs. A dog rested by the fire, and everything was quiet and in order, so it was not difficult for the couple to pluck up the courage to ask to be married. The man listened to the story of how they had met, and how they had discovered the sand on the beach, and how they had finally reached the point of choosing to be together, not just in time but unconditionally.

"But have you learned to breathe together?" he asked them. "You have made this choice, but have you breathed together? Have you allowed the universe to breathe through you?"

This was a startling question to them, for it was something they had never considered before. And so, although they had traveled far to find a man to marry them, the old man said, "I cannot marry you now . . . not until you go away and learn to breathe together in peace and in knowledge. When you have learned that, you may come and see me again." With that he turned back toward the fire, looking deep into the center of the flames where the azure blue emerges before the oranges and golds.

The couple turned and walked out into the sunlight. They returned to their home, still choosing to be together, and began to learn the art of breathing. They asked the trees and plants and flowers to reveal the secrets of the life breath. They listened to the hum of the bees as they pollenated the flowers and made honey, and began to feel the rhythms and cycles in the world of nature. They would grow quiet, and almost stop breathing themselves until they could listen to the breath of the universe. When they listened to their own hearts, they found the breath in their own bodies. Little by little they practiced the art of breath until one day when they both breathed out together, they realized that the universe was breathing them in at the same moment.

At that moment their world reversed and they found themselves in a space which they had not known before. They were being breathed by the universe. And so they understood about breath.

The couple traveled hand in hand in return to see the old man, convinced that now he would marry them, and at their arrival they presented him with gifts of honey and flowers, which he accepted with a kindly face. He gave them tea and sat by the fire as they told the story of their new realizations of the source of all breath, and what had happened to their bodies and how their love had taken on a different dimension. He smiled and listened carefully, and then asked them to listen carefully to him.

"So," he began, "you have started on the journey at last. You have learned to breathe together and in that study you have come upon certain things which mankind does not yet realize. You have made the first step toward fulfillment, but there are more steps. Breath alone is not enough."

Their hearts sank, because they had so hoped to be married, and now they were being told there was another test to be made. "But . . ." the young man began. "Don't argue with me," the old man said almost crossly. "You made the decision to be together, but you must fulfill certain obligations in taking on the responsibility of being man and woman, and that requires a certain knowledge. So you are brought to the second test. You have learned to breathe together—and now you must learn to sound the name of God together. Go. And when you have sounded His name together you may come back."

Once more the two turned into the sunlight wondering. What was the name of God, and why was it necessary for them to sound the name together?

For a long while they looked everywhere for the name of God, by searching through books and asking teachers. But the teachers just smiled and told them to meditate and ask for the name in their hearts. They sounded the names of the Hindu gods, and chanted the OM until their bodies resounded. They went through all the religions and sounded all the names of God that they could find. In the Bible they found the words, "When two or more are gathered together in my name, there am I in the midst of them." What was that name? They asked the sheikhs and learned the science of Wazifa, the repetition of the ninety-nine names of God, and they called on Allah until the sound was so sweet that wherever they went people would turn to them and smile at the light in their eyes and the presence of love they brought with them.

Then one day they watched a sunrise and heard a sound rising from the whole substance of the universe, and that sound brought the whole of creation bursting into life. Suddenly, from within that sound they heard His name. It was as though the whole universe responded to the sound or was nothing other than the manifestation of that name. The rocks sang, the trees swayed, and the birds and animals gathered around to be with them at this moment in which the Kingdom was revealed to them.

So they returned to the old man on a bright spring day with happiness overflowing in their hearts. The old man seemed surprised to see them since they had been gone so long, but he welcomed them warmly and sat with them by the open fire. "So?" He looked at them very carefully. "You have come upon His name!" It was not so much a question, but a statement of recognition, and all three sat close together, clasping each other's hands and there was a warmth in the room which permeated even the old stones of his humble cabin. "Now, please," they begged, "will you marry us?" They were eager with anticipation. There was a moment's silence and then the old man, taking their hands once again, looked deep into their eyes and said, "Dear friends, you have the first two tests. You have done well, but there is one more test that you must fulfill. Do not be disappointed or afraid, but the world has waited so long for this, and it is necessary that the last test that you must pass be understood by all mankind. You see, when you learned to breathe together, you learned how life is transmitted. When you learned to sound the name of God together you learned of the sound of the overflowing of the creation within God himself. Now you must learn *how*—you must learn how He does it. Go away, beloved friends, and learn how the Pyramids were made. When you have learned—and you will—then return and this time I will marry you."

It was a bitter disappointment, and yet, deep within their hearts, the couple knew that what the old man was saying was the truth and that, because of their choosing to be together, they were offered these strange tests, and this last one was, like the others, not just for them, but for all mankind.

They traveled all around, to the experts, and read books asking for the answer to the question: How had the pyramids been built? They gathered together a large amount of information, but still they did not have the knowledge that they needed.

Finally, they heard of a man who lived in a remote section of Wales, and they went off in search of him. At last it seemed that the end of their search was at hand as they climbed the last trail toward the farmhouse. Every fiber of their being was on fire with the yearning for fulfillment of their quest. But when they found the hut and knocked on the door a voice asked, "Who is there?"

"Please," they answered, "we have been looking so long for something and they say that you can provide us with the answer."

"Go away," he said. "There is no room for both you and me."

Then there was silence once more, and the couple sat down on the side of the mountain as the sun was setting and, not knowing what to do, they simply breathed together and sounded His name quietly together, and then, feeling better, they returned to the hut and again came the question, "Who is there?" This time they said quietly, "We have come to be with you." A pause and then a shout from within, "I told you, whoever you are, there isn't room in here for more than one . . . so go away. I don't want you here."

They were desperate. The sun had dropped over the hills and the moon and stars were coming out. So they went back to the place where they had breathed together and sounded His name together, and this time they began to pray. "Beloved Lord, whoever you are, wherever you are, please help us . . ." In silence they waited on through the night, and from time to time they heard a dog bark on the other side of the valley. Then in the moonlight they turned toward each other and embraced and walked back toward the hut. This time their knock received the same question from within, "Who is there?" "It is Thou, Thyself," they answered, and the door was opened. Then they saw the open fire and the dog by the grate, and the warmth permeated into their bodies. A wizened old man laughed and laughed as they entered, jumping up and down with laughter. He asked, "So what have you come for?"

They took a deep breath, and then together they asked him how the Pyramids were built. "Do you really want to know?" he asked.

Their hearts burst open like pomegranates in the sun, as they poured forth their story to him. He laughed and laughed and picked up two wooden balls which were tied on the ends of two pieces of string that were tied at the top. Then, screeching with laughter, he took hold of the joined ends of the string and by moving his arm, the two balls began to clap together. Click, click, click came the sound as he held the strings in his hand.

Then they knew! They kissed him, one on one cheek and one on the other as they left to walk through the moonlight under the stars.

It was morning when they reached the tiny village, and knocked on the old man's door for the last time. The village green was filled with jonquils. The birds were singing as never before, and they knew that they had reached the end of their journey.

The old man opened the door, his face all smiling, his hands outstretched. Three open hearts met in one, and turning toward them he said, "Today you will be married!"

As the sun rose to its zenith on that day in May, all the villagers assembled around the maypole, each one taking a different ribbon as the music played, and the villagers danced around, plaiting the different colors to weave the intricate diamond patterns into the maypole.

When the ceremony was over, there was a perfect pattern woven onto the pole, but when a little child came to touch the ribbons he found that the couple had already gone.

It was much later on that the villagers were asking where the old man was. He had not appeared for the great feast that had taken place after the ceremony and there was no sign of life in his little cottage. They went to try to find him, and finally opened the door. There was no one there. The fire was just left smouldering in the grate, the dog was nowhere to be seen, and as for the old man . . . had he ever existed?

No one ever came to find out the answer to that question, but after that time the maypole was taken down, the ribbons were buried, and the village became a place of pilgrimage. Every May Day, when the sun was at its zenith, people from all over the world came to sit quietly on the village green, and they would breathe together, and they would sound the name of God together, and they would smile as they took out two pieces of string joined together at one end, and with two weights at the other ends, they held them in their hands and heard the click, click, click, as they hit together . . .

THE SUFI AND HASSIDIC POINTS OF VIEW

THE SACRED FIRE

If husband and wife are deserving, God's presence dwells in their midst. If they are not deserving, fire devours them.

"For," said Rabbi Akiba, "the Hebrew word for man is *ish,* spelled aleph, yod, shin. Remove the yod and you have aleph shin, or *esh,* meaning fire. The Hebrew word for woman is *ishah,* spelled aleph, shin, heh. Remove the heh and, once again, you have *esh,* meaning fire.''

From this we learn that there is a consuming fire in the heart of every man and woman. When they marry, two fires are brought together that are capable of destroying whole worlds, if not properly tended. To quench that fire is impossible—for it generates the life of the world. But to leave the fire as it is also is impossible, for it generates evil as well.

What did God do? He placed one of the letters of His name, the first letter of the divine name, yod, between the aleph and the shin to make the Hebrew name for ''man.'' And he took the second letter of His name, the heh, and placed it after the aleph and the shin to make the Hebrew name for ''woman.'' In that way, both the man and woman retain in their names the word ''fire,'' but when they marry, the divine presence dwells in their midst, in the combination of their names. Wherever God's presence dwells, that fire gives warmth and heat, but it does not devour and consume. If husband and wife don't make the divine presence unwelcome, its blessing rests on the work of their hands and they become as partners in the act of divine creation. But if they make the presence unwelcome so that it does not dwell in their midst, they are left only with two consuming flames.

A. E. Kitov, The Jew and His Home (reprinted with
permission of Shengold Publishers, Inc., New York)

THE HASSIDIC POINT OF VIEW
REB ZALMAN SCHACHTER AND ELANA SCHACHTER

The dynamics of the marriage relationship is an opportunity to manifest the unity of God through the duality of two people. That exercise to maintain individuality and yet recognize unity is a very strong spiritual practice. Marriage is a situation in which you can't close your religious cycle within yourself. Your partner always brings in another dynamic point of view, another argument, another point of contention, another point of agreement, to broaden your scope. Although God is in me, God is also beyond me, and the manifestation of that beyondness always comes to me through my partner and to him through me.

Elana Schachter

In a relationship we can't play the bigger vs. the smaller, or the smaller vs. the bigger. On the level on which an act done for the other is really full, and calls for the total concentration of affection and attention and intention, then devotion is really very much there. That's why householders can do more than sanyasins [renunciate monks] in some aspects, because they have the chance to offer their love to one another and, through one another, to God.

Reb Zalman Schachter

In a spiritual marriage, the things you do don't have to necessarily be compatible, but there has to be respect on the part of both partners for what the other one is doing.

Even if it's not my particular trip, if it's important to Zalman, then, for no other reason than that, it's important to me. Hopefully, he can explain to me why it's important to him, so that it becomes important to me on more levels than just that it's important to him. So I would say, respect is one very important ingredient.

Both sharing time and private time are also very important. Sharing some

26

practice in common is particularly important. Some explicitly spiritual practice, be it a prayer practice, a mediation practice, a body discipline practice, or generally the experience of sharing as a basis for spiritual discussion, is the most important ingredient.

Elana Schachter

Many of the monastic spiritual disciplines seem to stress the hermit's way, but there are other ways which are between people. These are very rich and holy. Meeting the holy days in the seasons together as a couple is so fantastically rich, every day is an embodiment of a different spiritual space. How does it affect me? How does it affect you? How we blend with these things and spend holy time together is very important. For this reason ancient seers developed a *takkanah* [an improvement in practice], meaning an arrangement that husband and wife should spend at least one-quarter hour or one-half hour twice a week learning the same thing and discussing it. In this learning of a text together there is something that happens which is very special.

Reb Zalman Schachter

One thing in a relationship that is very important is to be able to live with one's partner's madness. There are people who normally are in a pretty good place, but when they get to their place of madness, to their lonely place, their upset place, they freak the other one out. It is very important to know what kinds of madness the other one is in. Can I love my partner in that madness too, in the right way? The right way often means not to interfere. It means not to take initiative away from the other one. On the other hand, one must know exactly where the support is needed and if and how it is available when the partner says, "I really can't do this one by myself; I need your help."

Another very important aspect is being able to give each other clear signals—weather reports. My wife, Elana, coined the phrase "weather report." It's giving a sense of what your emotional state is. If I see Elana isn't feeling good, she isn't shining, she isn't coming through with energy sometimes, I may get the feeling that it's due to something bad I did. Then a lot of hangups and guilt may come into the situation. It's better if the partner says, "Listen, I just happen to be out of sorts right now; it has nothing to do with you." Or, "if it has to do with you, it's because you did this and that." So we decided that we like it better even if we tend to be redundant—overstating on the signal, rather than not giving enough signal and reinforcing misunderstanding.

Reb Zalman Schachter

THE CREATIVE PROCESS OF LOVE
FROM A TALK BY PIR VILAYAT INAYAT KHAN

Love is the most creative thing that there is. Love itself is the reciprocally creative force for each mate who is involved in a true relationship, because in a true relationship love is really being infused at every moment through the qualities which one sees in one's partner.

According to the Sufis, a person is simply the custodian of these qualities which are actually divine qualities. One person exhibits more of certain qualities than others, and so it is a way of expressing one's worship of God to be infused by what comes through a person.

However, as one gets acquainted with a person, one does discover the personality features of a person which sometimes differ very much from their real spiritual being, which I call the seed. And that's where the conflicts arise; in fact, people are most surprised to find these things which they didn't expect, because they had seen only the ideal. These things have to be worked out, and one of the ways of doing it is to respect a person, which means to accept that person the way they are instead of trying to change him or her.

The other thing is that, in fact, by believing, envisioning the qualities of that person which you see in that person—I call it the seed of their personality—you help them to be themselves, their real being, because you believe in their real being.

And that's where love is so creative, where love becomes wonderful.

Now it is true that in a relationship one passes through a kind of crisis, because nothing can remain stagnant in life. And so, if you take each other for granted, your love starts to disintegrate. You have to keep on discovering one another, and you have to keep on changing your love. It can never remain the same. In fact, I would say that one has to be prepared to lose one's love in order to find it. That is, the thing that destroys the love relationship is for a person to feel possessed—nobody likes to be possessed, although there is the instinct in the human being to try to possess a person. That's what I mean when I say one has to really give one's love, not try to hold it. One has to be worthy of the relationship.

So I say, it is easy to love a person because they are wonderful, but the whole test of love is to love a person despite the fact that they do not live up to what one sees in them. There is necessarily a giving in a love relationship.

One of the best ways for the love relationship to progress is for it to gain in dimensions other than the purely personal ones. That's where a lot of love relationships are bogged down. When the relationship boils down to just babysitting, paying for car repairs and insurance, and performing all the daily chores, the couple does not have time to deal with each other and relate

to each other in a spiritual way. This is the time they may look for romance in some other person with whom they don't have the "kitchen sink" problems.

That's why a relationship is something that one really has to nurture, to culture. I mean, one takes time to water a plant and so on; it takes a lot of thought on one's part for a relationship to flourish.

The other thing is that it should gain new dimensions. This means that it should always be inspiring. That's why it is so important to speak about meditation and being high in the relationship. I think that there is nothing more wonderful in a relationship than being high, because by inspiring your partner you make the relationship deeper. If one or both of the partners is always caught up in his personality, it is a weight upon the relationship. The relationship becomes very difficult if people are just relating at the purely personal level.

So the only safeguard of a relationship is when one is able to meet the other at a very high level. One of the ways of doing it is to do practices together, spiritual practices, or even just talk about spiritual ideals. Of course, meeting on this high level means that there should be nothing that one can't talk about. One should be absolutely "up front" about how one feels about everything. I think even the planning of one's day has to be done in terms of one's spiritual ideals, and then one works it out in practice as to how one actually does it.

Uniting in this way is the only way in which a relationship is possible, because it is a tremendous *tour de force* for two wills to coordinate together. Sometimes one will is stronger than the other, and the one who gives in feels bad about it, becomes frustrated, and the other one continues to bully him or her. That makes a relationship very difficult. If the two wills are equally strong, then there is conflict. So the only way in which a relationship is possible at all is if both persons really relate so completely that there is no pressure exercised by one upon the other; both of them are inspired by their oneness. It is a feeling of being one person.

Really, a part of the New Age is the convergence of beings toward One Being. We are talking about the convergence at the level of humanity. The first stage is when two people begin to feel as though they are one being, they start saying the same things. One of the signs that they are converging is when they both start a sentence the same way; or, one thinks one thing and the other says it, and things like that. Then, when they are apart, they discover the person they love in themselves. They don't have to think of that person as being over there, because he or she is right inside them. That's where the love relationship becomes very inspiring.

IN PRAISE OF MARRIAGE AS A SPIRITUAL PATH
BY MURSHID SAMUEL LEWIS

There was a lull in the rainy season:
Jacarandas now could blossom without fear,
Creamy arjuna flowers made their appearance,
Fragrant jasmines scented the air,
Giant deodars shook, awakening from dreaming,
Bougainvilles colored every slope,
And the jungle donned its gayest plumage–
Birds responded: the hoopoe and cockatoo and pheasant,
And peacocks strutted around gardens,
With choruses of frogs and insects to form the battery.
Then I spent time wandering in the gardens,
Feeling myself part of the very earth,
I could see Parvati as she strolled,
So essential to the scene.

Could the music that so captivated animals
Appeal to the beloved of my heart and win her grace?
My Parvati seemed a million times more important
Than all the other beings in experience.

When I was young I had been affianced,
For it was the custom that everyone must marry;
Nor was there any great distinction between the sexes,
Though the education of the boy had been my lot,
And the education of the girl was otherwise.
Then there was no purdah, no seclusion
Excepting for one brief period at puberty
When tremendous new life surged into the flesh,
And it was wise to instruct the young accordingly.
Women were as free as men,
Though both were bound by custom—
We lived when wars were rare,
When peaceful relations were found more profitable,
And the young could marry without the community,
Although they could not affiance outside their gens.
So it was arranged that I meet with Parvati,
And instantly we admired one another.

We shared in various labors:
She with me in the hills, I with her in the home;
And I learned the ways of woman from her,
And she acquired the ways of man from me,
While youthful élan expressed itself in both:
In me in a positive manner, in her in a responsive manner,
So we dwelt together to test compatibility,
And as there was serenity, as there was joy,
Our marriage was sanctified by the community.

In the warm embrace of Parvati I found another music,
Felt the throbbing of supernal bliss.
Imagine a mighty organ with rows upon rows of pipes;
The shrill flute, the lisping vox humana,
The mighty bourdon and the deep diapason,
The proud trosha and the singing viols—
There are those, and many, many more.
As the organ is to the flute,
So the human expressions of love to those with animals,
And this experience of divinity in man,
Pictured as Kama Yoga, completion through desire,
But not to be differentiated from other yogas
Even though they are different to the uninitiated,
Is one way to the grand fulfillment of life.

We often visited the oracle,
A virgin of keen sight and humble mien,
Who saw beyond dense Prithivi,
Communed with spirits and even with gods,
This to read the language of the fated.
We never forced young maidens into strange wedlock
With those of deep maturity, or bearded hoodlums.
Marriage was a means toward higher evolution,
To fulfill some unexplored portion of karma,
Made for men and women working together.
Ah, to look down the course of centuries
To see the rites of marriage so polluted,
Legalities and conventions substituted,
The soul and God forgot and compulsions
Even for the sanctitude of the bed chamber.
We had no vested priesthood in those times,
Nor detailed legalisms fixating life,
Regarding all our children as souls,
Souls on a continuous journey from life to life.

What a wonderful beginning for new adventures,
For in loving Parvati I came to love the world,
And found in her that selfsame wonder
That I had learned in the vastness of the jungles.
To me the wife was more than miracle,
To me the wife became more than an imagined divinity,
To me the wife was more than all my faculties,
That before our marriage I had known only half-life;
Now there was fulfillment of every part of personality.
Man needs God to become complete, and woman also;
But the male may discover divinity in the female,
And the female may encounter completion in the male.

Then indeed does marriage become a communion,
Then is every interaction sacred:
Communion in sharing worldly goods,
Communion in joy and sorrow and tribulation,
Communion in physical function and in devotion,
Parvati and I became as one,
Husband and wife, wife and husband were as one;
As the days passed, so the years passed,
Only our bodies and minds remained apart,
So every act between us was a sacrament,
In giving, in doing, in completing our marriage.

What had man for woman:
Above all that power which arises out of space,

Which originates in the deep springs of the universe,
Which formulates the motifs of the male,
Makes for his prowess and protecting hand,
Passes through his sinews into his loins,
As Lingam-Shakta incarnate.
I poured my essence into my woman
That she might share the virtue of those facilities.
And what, in turn, had she for me?
Above all, that magnetism which springs from earth,
Which emanates from atoms, from the essence of thingness,
Responsive, healing, cooling, revivifying.
These virtues circulate throughout her being,
Combine with many rhythms drawn from earth,
And from her came blessings I might share—
This Yoni-Shakti, the assimilation of life in things,
Which transforms a corpse into a thing of beauty.

O Kama! Kama! What perfidies commited in thy name!
Love befouled by passion in fancy or fact.
Love besmirched by decrepit lust-desire,
Love made into everything—but love.
But knowing the real spirit of the universe,
Understanding the all-propelling nature of this urge,
I saw that sex and marriage are pathways to divinity,
Upward, if traveled in harmony with nature,
Upward, if personal duties were fulfilled,
When sharing, giving, taking are regarded as sacred.
Even our half-bodies are no longer obstacles,
Our imperfections become as meaningless,
When the science-art of Kama Yoga is practiced.

> And when at last my course was run,
> When my work on earth was done,
> When departing from this life
> Leaving behind beloved wife;
> My spirit did not rise above,
> Held by the noble bond of love,
> Which raised Parvati's eyes to mine,
> Her heart repeating "I am thine";
> She then prepared the funeral pyre,
> Threw her bones upon consuming fire,
> Indifferent to the burning flame,
> Feeling my absence a greater shame,
> She would not stay half-dead, bereft,
> All life had gone when I had left,
> Her glory was to be with me,
> Heart linked to heart, eternally.

from *Siva! Siva!*

II
PERSONAL EXPERIENCES: The Husband-Wife Relationship

One day my wife, Abha, and I were sitting really close to Babaji [Baba Hari Dass]. Suddenly I felt an indescribably beautiful feeling, and I just looked at Babaji and blurted out, "She's my Earth Mother," referring to Abha. Babaji looked at me very calmly and wrote, "Yes, as you are her God Father." I felt I should write this down and put it on the wall so that every time we have an argument I will remember who we are.

Mahesh Naud

WHAT IS THE SPIRITUAL PURPOSE OF MARRIAGE?

Marriage is hard sadhana. Its intimacy offers opportunities for spiritual growth not usually afforded by other interpersonal relations. There are also karmic purposes.

George McClure

To glorify God by obeying His word, to become one as man and wife, and to be fruitful. To raise up children whose lives spiritually, as well as physically, glorify God.

Hilda Pickering

SPEAKING FROM EXPERIENCE
EXCERPTS FROM AN INTERVIEW WITH STEPHEN AND INA MAY GASKIN

RD: Where are you at now concerning marriage, and how did you come to be there?

S: Before I came to *know,* I'd been a lot of other places; a lot of different kinds of other places. I was married to a girl when I was twenty-one, when I was going to college. It lasted two years. We never had kids, and I don't even know where she is any more. We were both just pitifully young. We lasted a couple of years because our folks would have gotten mad if we had broken up the first time we got mad at each other. And then another girl for five years and we had a kid. And from that I had the experience of being separated. The kid's fifteen years old now, just going back and forth between me and that lady. In six-month or nine-month or one-year intervals, she changes back and forth from that lady's house to me. That was a heartache to go through—that change.

But now if somebody comes up to me and says, "Man, my old man is going to go get a lawyer and take custody of my kid if I come live on The Farm," I say, "Man, my daughter went to this other tribe and I didn't dig their ways. And I kept my mouth shut for years and years and years. Just in order to keep peace. And waited. And she's fifteen years old and she loves me and I love her and we're friends and we're tight. Just as good, maybe more than if we lived in the same household. And she's had another whole raft of experience, and she's a very open-ended kid. I look into her and the back of her head falls out; there's something out the other end that I didn't do." It's kind of far-out in a way. On this end she's my kid, and on that end she's somebody else's. It's a deep relationship, and it makes me able to handle that.

A lot of hippies break up, man. A lot of hippies break up. And there are a lot of kids that aren't with their right parents and all that kind of stuff, and The Farm has accepted that karma; we welcome it. It just seems like the answer now is no longer seeking the dharma or knowing the dharma. It's living the dharma. That's just really living where it's at, is living the dharma.

I've got five kids now. And then I've got two that I took, that some folks gave away. I've got my own girl, and my wife's daughter by a previous marriage, and then our three all born on The Farm. And then I've got two—aged thirteen and eleven—who I adopted. When I first met them they were a little neurotic and a little weird, you know—but with a little love and letting them fold out and come out, they're just amazing. Beautiful, beautiful children, and I'm very much in love with both of them, and they're in love with me; and we've got a bond the same as or as good as but a different flavor.

RD: Can you give some direct advice to couples who are working on their relationships?

S: In the course of the changes I have gone through, I learned to give ladies their space. And the first time that I ever really did it, it scared me, because I had to back up so far. I had to back up and back up and back up. I mean like not being up in somebody's free will; not messing around with somebody's free will; some human being's own, God-given, karma-free, free will. I had so many opinions.

I don't think that's just from the man's side. I think it's from the woman's side too. I think two human beings have to learn to give each other free will and not manipulate each other. . . . It's like saying, "If you think it is neat when you catch somebody, wait until you hit somebody who is coming the other way just as hard as you are."

Another thing is: you can't argue your way out of a head trip; you can't think your way out of a head trip.

RD: Ina May, what advice could you offer to couples involved in making their marriage relationships more meaningful?

IM: Well, you have that heavy flash that this is who I want to be with; this is it. But you can't expect that flash will happen every day and just hang back and wait for the romantic excitement to sweep you over all the time. Love is something that you have to make. You have to create it; you don't just hang around complaining how it ain't like it used to be. If it isn't, better do something about it. Better get off your butt and figure out what it's going to take. Sometimes you just need to talk. You need to put out some energy in some form; you need to figure out what form it should take.

Another thing, children get the most basic attitude in the early years of their lives. It can be changed, but it's really important what you put in there. If a relationship isn't making it, it's important to work it out, come to some kind of agreement where you're going to agree with whatever it is. If you're going to stay or not going to stay together. Don't string it out for a long time. For the kids.

EXCERPT FROM AN INTERVIEW WITH GURU RAJ SINGH AND GURU RAJ KAUR

RD: In your marriage relationship, let's say one of you gets angry. How do you deal with that?

GRK: Guru Raj Singh has a way of withdrawing instead of outwardly showing anger, whereas I get angry and lash out.

RD: So your patterns are different.

GRS: I don't pay too much attention to her, really, when she gets mad at me. I try not to feel it very much; sometimes it works and sometimes it doesn't.

GRK: What makes me angry, as a woman, is if I feel my creative energy is being rejected. If I'm trying to give in some way, and it's not accepted by my husband, my tendency is to want a reaction, so I'll get angry. When I do that, I find that the best thing for him to do is to stay neutral about the whole thing, and not to get wrapped up in it. He's really good at that; somehow he is often able, in a transcendent way, just to say "Hey, what are you doing?"

RD: He's seeing through your mood, making some space for you so that you can see what your trip is, whether you're hanging on.

GRK: Right. And Guru Raj Singh's way of showing insecurity is to become pessimistic and extreme, and say things like, "Well, forget everything." He's never said that about our marriage; it usually has to do with a project that's important to us; I have to just laugh about it, stay light, and know that the moment's going to pass. We haven't often both been into the depths of negativity at the same time. We find that when one of us is going through changes, the other has to transcend in order to help out; as long as that happens, everything's fine.

GRS: It's like being on a seesaw. One partner can't get off. It goes up and down, and that's what it's for.

RD: There is a tremendous security in a marriage like this, when you have the space to freak out, and know that your mate isn't going to feed it too much. You know and trust that essence, and really follow that through, all the way.

GRS: Because you didn't get married to all that guck. You married in the essence.

GRK: In the marriage we're involved in, as directors of this ashram, one hassle has been an inability to spend any time with each other. There are two extremes with that. On the one hand, we realize our work is more important than our marriage; we're the last priority. On the other hand, we sometimes work so hard that we don't get to spend *any* time together.

I would give any married couple just a little bit of advice: no matter how devoted you are to your work, to your dharma and your sadhana, do spend time with your husband or wife, and with your family; spent right, it makes a basic foundation of security. Just to sit together, or go for a walk together, or to sleep together—that can be enough.

RD: There are rituals that families can do together. Like, for example, the Jewish sabbath or the Hindu arti. Even eating supper together and holding hands and saying grace. Simple stuff like that. Just to get that feeling of "Well, here we are." Ways of developing that "usness" feeling.

GRS: It's wonderful to develop the sensitivity to feel when that high polarity is going to come, when the best is going to come, when you should share; then you can disperse again. If you don't have that high time together, then it's like having a garden which is nicely trimmed, fertilized, and pruned; everything is properly cared for, and you can even sit and chant to the flowers, but if there's no water, nothing's going to grow.

GRK: Another basic thing about marriage is this: you're not getting married in order to complement yourself or supplement yourself. Marriage is two *complete* entities giving to one another. The idea is not to get married because you think, "Oh, I'm lacking this and I'm lacking that." Marriage is a full vessel, overflowing to give to the partner. You marry to give, not to take.

RD: I think I know what you're saying. It is very important; I think the overwhelming thing that is happening with many people is that basically they feel insecure, they are not happy, they feel empty. Then they look to the outside for help.

GRK: Women often *want* something to be dependent on, a way of security; to have someone to provide for them. And then the man is looking for the ultimate mother, upon whom he can rest his head. There is some truth in this, but it is very tricky.

Yogiji [spiritual leader of the 3HO organization] says again and again that in a marriage you can't live *against* the person; there cannot be thoughts like "I have my space and you have yours; don't bug me." Then there's also the fallacy that simply living *with* each other can work: "Well, we'll kind of blend whenever we can." Yogiji says that won't work either. You have to *live for* each other. That encompasses many small and large sacrifices that one has to be prepared to make.

RD: Something that Bubba Freejohn said comes to mind. He said that anybody who's been really married will tell you that marriage is a tapas [purification by fire]. I think that's what you're saying: marriage is tapas, in the sense of sacrifice and austerity.

GRS: We had some marriages recently in our ashram, and Yogiji was here to perform them. He gave us about a forty-five-minute talk on marriage. He was expressing himself in very powerful, vivid terms. He wasn't pulling any punches at all. He was chopping off everybody's head left and right. It was one of the most powerful talks I have ever heard him give on marriage, and after he finished talking we left immediately for another talk. I was driving. I said to him. "Oh boy, Yogiji, I sure have a headache." He said, "Yeah, you're not kidding you have a headache. Anybody who listened to that talk who is married has got to have a headache." That's the tapas.

I have seen him perform a wedding ceremony in which he sits in front of the couple and he says, "I am sorry, I am not going to marry you." Their parents have come from thousands of miles away, the cake is baked, the flowers are threaded—everything is done. He says, "I am sorry. Unless you can justify yourselves in a certain way, I am not going to marry you." And he'll ask a specific question—I have seen him do it several times. He'll ask a specific question to the husband, like, "If she has a child, what are you going to do with it?" Well, the husband is only thinking about saying "I do." But Yogiji is perceiving something, some potentiality somewhere. . . . This man could abuse a child, or would not value that child, somehow. And he's going to make that conscious before he's going to tie the knot. He really would get up and leave the ceremony if the right answer didn't come. The tapas begins right there.

EXCERPTS FROM AN INTERVIEW WITH
BARRY AND JOYCE VISSELL

J: Barry and I have had much experience and training working with couples and individuals, Barry in medical school and psychiatry training, and me in nursing and graduate school, and also both of us have had training in many of the newest therapies. However, the most important, and really the only experience that we feel gives us qualification to work with couples is that we have been together for thirteen years and we love each other ever more deeply day by day. We believe in the beauty of a close, lasting, and committed one-to-one relationship. As I love Barry ever more deeply, so am I able to love God ever more deeply. Loving, appreciating, adoring, and seeing the presence of God in Barry allows me to feel God and beauty in myself and others. I truly am happiest when I see the light shining through his eyes. We used to feel that the other would get ahead on the spiritual path, but now we see that neither makes it before the other and we go hand in hand and step by step together toward the One goal.

RD: How do you get people to appreciate each other? I'm just wondering how that can be drawn out when a couple is at the point of visiting a counselor?

B: We have them face each other often, especially some couples who come and will sit and face us and never look at each other. We pick that up right away. So we physically turn them around and point their bodies toward each other, and have them make eye contact and have them maybe stop talking for a bit. Quiet down, look at each other, tune in to the deepest place within this person. Look past the eyes, look past the face, look at the soul, feel that closeness that is there. It's always there. Sometimes it has to be almost like a meditation, we have to guide them. Sometimes we just have to have them start appreciating. Because sometimes people have never done it. They've been together as a couple for who knows how long, and they've never really appreciated the other person. When we have them do it, sometimes it starts out with ''I like your hair,'' or . . . sometimes it's physical appreciation and then it gets deeper.

RD: Things that a lot of people are scared to admit. I know a lot of people who are afraid to admit negative things, but they're just as afraid to admit positive things to each other. It's really hard to say to somebody ''I love you.''

J: There is a very very important point to get across to people about appreciation. Many partners in relationships are looking to be appreciated rather than to appreciate—wanting to be loved rather than to love. One of the most basic spiritual laws is *to give,* for only by giving of one's self can one expand and receive. The one who is appreciating the other really is the one gaining the most. To receive the love we are wanting we must first give it out.

One of the most beautiful things we do in our relationship now—and what we work with other couples on—is feeling the presence of the other. By this I mean feeling the higher self or God-self of your partner, feeling those attributes that you dearly love in this other being. I feel so beautiful myself when I can feel the higher aspect of Barry— when I can feel his deep love, understanding, wisdom, and gentleness. Our work is to ignore each other's personality more and tune into the higher self of each other and ourself. This is very freeing for us both. Many times couples who come to us have a hard time with this, especially when they are in each other's physical presence. So I go with the woman to another room, and Barry works with the man. I begin by having the woman talk about why she is with the man to begin with—what it was that attracted her. Then I have her recall times when he seemed so beautiful and it was easy to see the higher self and the higher attributes. It starts out mental, then we bring it into the feelings. We meditate together then and feel these higher attributes of our partners. It's very beautiful and many times within just ten or fifteen minutes the woman is deeply feeling her love. Often when we return to the men they are still in the mental plane, and many times all the man has to do is look at his wife beaming love at him and he goes to his heart, also able to do the same. We are then all reminded how simple and beautiful divine love is and we feel like children. Many couples practice this at home in separate rooms or together, and are more and more able to contact the higher aspect of the other.

An extremely important part of a relationship is in not taking the other for granted. Sometimes we see a couple when they first fall in love. There is so much love and respect and they commit themselves to each other and vow to hold onto this beautiful spark of love. Then we see them sometimes less than a year later and they sadly announce that the spark went out and they feel in a rut with each other. The spark never goes out, but it needs to be fed. It takes work and the self-discipline of old habits to not take the other for granted and lose respect. We find that meditating separately and together helps a tremendous amount. During these periods of stillness, seeing the beauty in the other and giving deepest thanks to God for the privilege of sharing your life with this person, realizing it is one of life's greatest blessings—this should be done at least once a day and, ideally, many many times. Sharing life so closely with another can be ever new joy and ever new beauty—we just need to put our attention there.

B: Not too long ago, in our work with couples, the emphasis was often on the relationship, the communication process, etc. And so it was with Joyce and me. We verbally expressed to each other just about every thought and feeling that came through. Partly it was our training . . . giving ultimate validity to all feelings, positive or negative. This is what happens with so many couples on the path. Although the ideal of intimate sharing is there, the result is inevitably a loss of individuality. Boy, are we all learning! There were actually times when Joyce and I would be meditating together, and it would be so beautiful . . . then maybe Joyce would get up to go to the bathroom to pee, and I couldn't continue meditating because of my dependence on her energy to sustain me.

So many couples, very beautiful beings, come to us and are almost totally unaware of how much they lean on each other. It manifests outwardly as blame, anger, criticism, jealousy, and on and on. Joyce and I have had some whopping fights, by the way, because of all this. If couples could only see that every time a feeling of irritation arises, it literally spells out unconscious dependency or leaning upon the one the feelings are directed toward. Make it conscious, recognize it for what it is. Once leaning is recognized—not in someone else: that's too easy; but in yourself—then, and only then, are you free to choose not to give power to anger. Believe me, it seems nothing less than a miracle in our relationship to see this all happening so fast. We're all on the path of mastery. Now, it really doesn't matter if a couple comes together to us, or if one comes alone. In fact, even when a couple comes together, we often see them individually, at least for part of the time . . . especially when the leaning on each other is unconscious, and when anger vibes fly between them like sparks. Very little can be accomplished under these closed conditions. So we may send one outside, or Joyce will work with one and I with the other. And then very beautiful things sometimes happen, even after they get back together again.

We each are an individualized presence of God, a single ray of light from the Great Central Sun of the universe. How thankful I am to finally begin to feel this wondrous truth. More and more, my first and only responsibility is to call upon God within me, the Christ, the "I Am" presence, the higher self, whatever you want to call it. A "spiritual marriage" or relationship can only be successful when the emphasis is on feeling the presence of God first.

Solitude is so very important. How hard it was initially for me to meditate alone. And, boy! do I remember those first solitary retreats, with no one else to blame for my lack of discipline. But, oh, how rewarding! How strengthening! And I don't mean taking a vacation away from your mate filled with distractions. There comes a time when you only want to "get on with it," and that means self-control, mastery of habit patterns—but especially feeling God and God only, in yourself and everyone else.

There is no need to share every thought and feeling with each other. Far better to keep silent most of the time. Now often the most beautiful "work" on our relationship gets done in silence, and often alone in meditation.

You talked about psychotherapy. There has been such a major switch in us, because I used to be the "psychiatrist," the doctor who was treating "patients" and effecting changes. I felt I was the one who was doing something to help this person. Now all we do is practice feeling God within, and therefore seeing God in him or her. And as deep as we go within, that's how much we're stepping aside and letting the "power" come through—and sometimes absolutely transcendent things happen. Then all we can do is thank God inwardly and thank the person outwardly.

Oh, thank God for the most precious gift of my life, for the miracle of entering into divine service with beloved Joyce as twin flames of the "Most High Living God."

CYCLIC "REMARRIAGE"
ACCORDING TO THE JEWISH TRADITION
EXCERPTS FROM AN INTERVIEW WITH
MORDECHAI AND HANA WOSK

H: The Hebrew word for marriage is *kedushin.* This comes from the root word *Kedosh,* which means holy or sacred. It is a word which is used to describe God. This shows us the Jewish perspective on marriage— that it is holy, a way of coming closer to God.

Mankind is described in the Torah as created in God's image. By entering into marriage a couple can come closer to actualizing this "likeness" to God. When, through their love, they create a new being, they are sharing in God's creative act. Just as God creates the world, we too are commanded to create. This is the first commandment which man and woman are given in the Torah—"Be fruitful and multiply."

The Torah gives guidelines which help to make marriage holy. Just prior to the marriage ceremony, the woman immerses in water which comes from a natural source. This is called *mikveh* in Hebrew. Every year I come to a new understanding as to what the *mikveh* means. It definitely seems to be a kind of rebirth experience. Going into the water is something like going into a womb and recognizing that the source of life is something beyond you. It's from God.

And only after you've gone through this immersion in the cosmic universal life energy, only then are you ready to unite sexually. It keeps you in a certain perspective. You might think that *you* are creating the next generation. You realize that it's not coming from yourselves, but that you are a part of something that's going through you.

M: Another guideline which the Torah gives a married couple is the rhythm of their sexual interaction. It is based on a physical rhythm which follows the menstrual cycle. And it also helps to establish an emotional, intellectual, and spiritual rhythm. The relationship can be described by the phrase *achoti kalah,* "my sister, my bride" [from the Song of Songs]. It works like this:

The sister part of the relationship between a man and a woman begins when the woman's menstrual period starts. This is a time for the couple to be apart sexually according to the Jewish law. After the flow stops they wait for an additional seven days. Then the woman immerses in the *mikveh,* just as prior to the marriage. After this complete cycle of time elapses, the couple moves out of the brother-sister relationship and back into the husband-wife relationship. Then, in a sense, the husband and wife remarry—they come together in physical union in their bride-and-groom relationship which continues for the rest of the month.

RD: So in other words the woman has an added responsibility for their sex life—it's not the husband's place to "come on" to the woman. It's up to the woman to accept that position.

Let's say that all is not right in the relationship. Even though this is her responsibility the woman can say, "I'm not going to fulfill my responsibility." That is something that can happen quite easily, right?

H: Yes.

M: It's a type of etiquette, a spiritual etiquette, to allow the woman to set the pace. When she's ready to be entered, she'll let you know.

RD: I guess the reason I brought this up is that in this culture I think it's almost always the man who's the aggressor and what you have presented here is just the reverse of that. But here the man is instructed to wait, be patient, to trust his wife, to give her that responsibility, and trust her—that she's going to let him know when the time is right.

H: The idea of the brother-sister relationship is, I think, one of building the strength of the individuals. I really feel the value of that space.

During this phase of the relationship the partners support each other, to develop their individuality, to experience their uniqueness in the world. A strong couple is made up of two strong individuals. It's a time for transmutation of sexual energy. Perhaps for working through emotional blocks, developing the intellect (i.e., by learning scriptures), spending more time in meditation.

During this brother-sister phase, sexual energies tend to recharge. This enhances the couple's appreciation and enjoyment of each other at the time of their reunion. The two individuals remerge into one. This rhythm keeps the relationship alive and charged, like that of a bride and groom.

III

TOWARD DIVINE LOVE

SEX AND SPIRITUALITY

When is ''one'' said of a man? When he is male together with female and is highly sanctified and zealous for sanctification; then and only then he is designated one without mar of any kind. Hence a man and his wife should have a single inclination at the hour of their union, and the man should be glad with his wife, attaching her to himself in affection. So conjoined, they make one soul and one body; a single soul through their affection; a single body, for only when male and female are conjoined do they form a single body; whereas, and this we have learned, if a man is not wedded, he is, we may say, divided in two. But when male and female are joined, God abides upon ''one'' and endows it with a holy spirit; and, as was said, these are called the children of the Holy One, be blessed.

Gershom G. Scholem, Zohar–The Book of Splendor (reprinted by permission
of Schocken Books Inc., copyright © 1949 by Schocken Books)

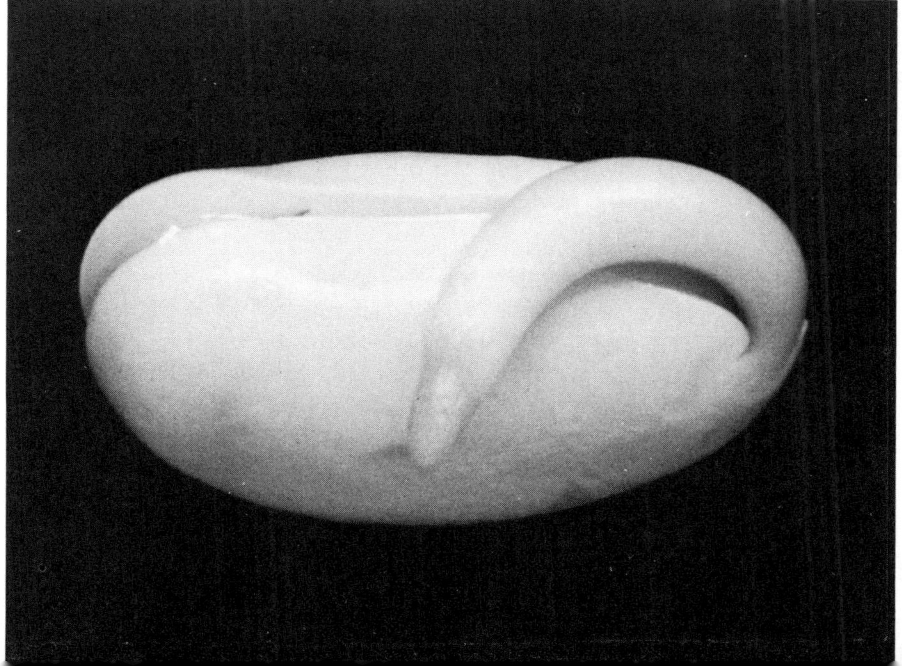

THE THREE "ABODES"

Probably the best terminology there is for the transcendental possibilities opened to us by sex is the Sufi one of the "abodes," though we must remember that here, any language has at best an indicative value, for our spiritual nature is inevitably beyond the reach of all of our ordinary faculties.

In Sufism, going back particularly to the teachings of the Kwajagan, the Masters of Wisdom, more than to any other branch of Sufism, the degrees of union are thought of as three abodes, *beit,* or dwellings in man. These can be said to be in the heart of man, in the depth of his own feeling nature, which is hidden from the reach of his ordinary emotions. The first abode is called the "Beit-ul-Muharem." *Muharem* means private, interior, or hidden, and comes from the same root as harem, which is the hidden place in the house where strangers do not enter. As I have said, our nature is incomplete. To become complete we require union with the other sex. The true union, which is more than an event in the physical world—marriage in the real sense of the word—is an act of will, a decision which consists in the mutual acceptance by a man and woman of each other. The Beit-ul-Muharem is the place where man and woman come together in this union, which is the true goal of sexual life.

It is only through the unconditional acceptance of the other that we come to the wholeness that is marriage. When one has any kind of reservation and bargaining, and one says that "I will put myself second in all except in this respect where I am better or I know better," then this acceptance is not possible. Complete acceptance does not mean subordination, nor does it mean blinding oneself to the weaknesses or defects of the other. If one did, it would not be acceptance: we must accept with our eyes open. This acceptance is a real discipline, and like the will of which it is a manifestation, it is only acquired gradually. When people talk to me and ask me about marriage, I simply say that if they wish their marriage to become a spiritual union, they must set themselves always to put the other first and themselves second; unless this is constantly practiced, they will not come to the Beit-ul-Muharem.

John G. Bennett, Sex (published by Coombe Springs Press, reprinted
by permission of the trustees of the late John G. Bennett)

SEX AND SUFISM
BY MURSHID MOINEDDIN JABLONSKI

"Toward the One, the perfection of love, harmony, and beauty, the only Being." This is how the invocation of the modern Sufi movement, founded early in this century by Hazrat Inayat Khan, begins. Unity, oneness, is the key for all endeavors that a Sufi may attempt, including attempts to be harmonious and affectionate with members of the same or opposite sex as in social situations, or to actually unify as in the case of human sexual consummation between couples. Questions of legal marriage aside, it is this recognition, appreciation, and love for a Thou that tends to complete desire, whether it be of the body or mind or heart or soul or all of these. A Sufi looks at simple bodily desire generally as a factor to be overlooked, overcome, or sublimated in the normal flow of his or her social life. Obviously, we must eat and exercise, so what I am referring to here is primarily the sexual urge when I speak of bodily desire.

However, as God created all, including our bodies, and saw that it was good, to His satisfaction, *tor* as the Bible says, there must be a proper sphere for human sexual activity. Some traditional religious outlooks have limited this activity to the basic continuance of the race, to procreation. Yet, there are other religious outlooks equally as sacramental, and perhaps more so, which permit, condone, and even encourage the love relationship to flower through a combination of scientific and devotional endeavors with a partner of the opposite sex, if I understand the elements of the *Kama Sutra* rightly. This is perhaps similar to forms of what is called *tantra*, a word no doubt as abused and misused as our own word *love* in this day of spiritual explosion.

Murshid Samuel Lewis, the late Sufi teacher from San Francisco, said tantra was simply to treat your mate like a god or goddess. That was the easiest definition. But while a Sufi overlooks, overcomes, or sublimates the sexual urge in the course of daily social life, there is definitely a marriage bed, there is definitely a period of time given over to the enjoyment of husband for wife, and of wife for husband. Yet this is just the husk, so to speak, which encloses a much vaster field of love. For the Sufi, love does not stop with the physical. Indeed, it may be true to say that a sort of mental consideration actuates the physical inclination. Whatever physical enjoyment there may be, doubtless the mental enjoyment is much greater, or perhaps the enjoyment of the body-mind, to use a Buddhist term, is more properly indicated here.

Since we are speaking primarily of joy and of love, it would be best to look even further in seeking a source of this love and joy, which source a Sufi is supposed to seek constantly. The *Taitteriya Upanishad* posits human joys as fairly low on the scale of cosmic evolution, and certainly sex may be regarded as one of the human joys. True, there are many examples of subhuman behavior which pass for joy and love as advertised on the marquees of North Beach and the Tenderloin, but these subhuman traits are not components basic to sexuality; they are, rather, components of ego and self-indulgence.

In one of the Sufi prayers, we say, "Raise us above the denseness of the earth," and even in the midst of the physical act of love a Sufi may be experiencing emotions and stimuli far beyond the usual range of the human sensorium, far beyond the norms of the ordinary man or woman. This is what happens when the heart of the beloved is regarded as a sacred and holy shrine.

Historically, Sufism has appeared against the background of Islam, and Sufis have tried to emulate the behavior of the prophet Mohammed, peace be upon him. Now, as we know from historical records, Mohammed not only was married, he had several wives after Kadeja died, and even condoned polygamy, if a man could be equal minded. Basically, Islam was given as a religion for humanity, and Mohammed certainly exemplified a well-integrated life, taking on the roles of warrior, statesman, prophet, husband, father, friend.

Thus, it can be seen that Mohammed presented the Divine Message replete with the possibility of making every aspect of life holy. Here, the Sufi would have to say that the "good" God of the puritanically minded pales in comparison with the perfect God amidst the entire gamut of life as we know it, from mineral and vegetable to the animal and human stages, and beyond. Who even permits crime and abnormal behavior to a certain extent, so that the possibility of perfection and its attainment from whatever level is assured. Nothing normal to a full life is left out.

But, frankly, it would be difficult to say there is any one approach to the subject of sexuality and Sufism. As Sufism is as varied as the sheikhs, murshids, and pirs who represent it, so are the approaches as varied as the couples who seek perfection through the uniqueness of their relationships. Murshid Samuel Lewis once said, "Sufis are not so scientific as the tantric people. Sufis simply keep their minds on God and their hearts filled with love."

Lofty symbolism aside, the Song of Solomon in the Old Testament is a good example of how a Sufi would approach the whole love relationship of which we are speaking. Yet, by virtue of the ideal involved, of the modesty with which the sacrament of marriage is culminated, the experience is lofty, and the poetry of it is felt right to the physical.

I think the best thing to say here is that a Sufi desires to integrate and synthesize the planes of body, heart, and soul into the Divine Presence, no matter what activity he or she is engaged in, be it sex, cooking, weaving, dancing, or anything. And it would be safe to say also that as the anatomical importance of the sex organs is small compared with the rest of the body, so a Sufi treats the time and place for sex as important, but never too much out of proportion to the larger body of life's activities that await solution, and through which a Sufi's overall dharma is fulfilled. Murshid Samuel Lewis has taught the problem of life is not to be solved through sex, but the solution of the problem of life and of sex is the same thing.

Celibacy is also practiced by Sufis, yet it is a practice undergone for the specific purpose of awakening the inner life during the period of spiritual seclusion known as khilvat. But khilvat is not regarded by Sufis as the supreme mode of life, especially as Mohammed declared, "Let there be no monkery in Islam." Rather, it is a specific time set aside for intensive inner work so that the disciple can return to society and better conduct the supreme practice of integrating the inner and outer life.

Besides celibacy, fasting and other austerities are combined with a program of constant spiritual practice. Khilvat might roughly be compared with the Zen practice of sesshin as to purpose, although sesshin is undertaken with a group, while khilvat is solitary. There may be isolated examples of Sufis, or even scattered branches of a Dervish brotherhood here and there, which have adopted a regular policy of celibacy, but this is perhaps more out of regard for the example of Jesus Christ as their chief ideal, rather than Mohammed, who has been and remains the exemplar for most of the traditional Sufi orders.

On the other hand, celibacy is a principle which may also come naturally to a Sufi as he or she advances on the spiritual path, and rises gradually above the concerns of humanity. Hazrat Inayat Khan presents this scene in his book *Rasa Shastra, the Science of Life's Creative Forces,* where he outlines the propensities of the desire-nature at various stages of the evolution of the ego. The lowest developed ego is, for example, concerned only with the self-centered gratification of physical appetites, while the next stage begins to show some little consideration for others. Finally, through successive stages, the higher developed ego begins to live only for his or her ideal, and every day becomes more aware of the feelings of others and sees the noble purpose of life.

FIDELITY

QUESTION: IS FIDELITY NECESSARY IN MARRIAGE?

Traditionally I have felt that it was desirable but not necessary. Yet all the great teachers proscribe infidelity, so therefore fidelity is "necessary" if one is to live by faith in the authority of these teachers. The biological-social basis for these teachings is that infidelity creates emotional tensions which impair the effectiveness of family and social units. *The spiritual basis may be that infidelity represents a distraction or running away from one's real sadhana and a false and superficial solution to the problems that must be faced in all marriages.* Infidelity is also a terrible trap in that it offers the illusion, the hope, of sexual satiation which is impossible without degradation.

George McClure

Absolutely. Because the bond between Christ and God is one of fidelity and oneness and is the basis for marriage. Once joined in marriage, the couple becomes one—where, then, is there room for infidelity?

Hilda Pickering

Yes. I've learned the lesson that if we are to share our lives together, in all manifestations, this precludes the possibilities of having experiences with another. You've got to be straight with your partner—and fidelity is the bond. Making it with others is just playing out a game with oneself, and leaves one, as Baba Hari Dass succinctly puts it, "always hungry."

Tom Kopka

TALKING FROM EXPERIENCE
EXCERPT FROM AN INTERVIEW WITH STEPHEN AND INA MAY GASKIN

RD: Would you share with us some of your attitude changes regarding fidelity and monogamy?

IMG/SG: What's happening on The Farm now is that we're being purely monogamous. We have come to this from a few years of trying to hold together things that didn't hold together very well. We have learned that what love holds together will hold together and what love does not hold together will not be held together.

We haven't given up our concept of extended family. We just feel that human beings seem to have a biological and psychological need for fidelity. And we see people who say, "Oh, I'm having such a good time banging around laying a lot of people." And they have four rows of bags under their eyes and you can see through their skin like parchment. They are not doing well. They have not settled their soul, which is starved to settle with someone and go deep into someone. And this doesn't happen on "one-night stands." When the going gets rough, they move on. When the time comes for the first test of the friendship, they break up.

MONOGAMY
BY HAZRAT INAYAT KHAN

Any study of psychology shows that success and happiness in life are found in singleness of mind. To focus itself the mind takes a single direction; and singleness of vision cannot fail to develop singleness of purpose. Many are the paths that lead to success; the difficulty lies in keeping strictly to the chosen path or, in other words, retaining singleness of mind. There is one means only by which man can attain to a realization of the religious ideal of the Godhead, and that is through sincerity and single-mindedness in the conduct of everyday life.

So it is that the ideal of monogamy has been considered by the wise as no less sacred than religion. In this ideal, verily, is found the natural law of religion.

Even among polygamous peoples monogamy prevails; because the one who is bound to several in marriage is most often devoted to one alone, and thus monogamy is in a sense more natural than polygamy. It is a tendency that is seen to a certain extent in birds and beasts. Doves, for instance, when mated remain attached to each other and share equally the responsibility of rearing their young. Many other animals always keep to one mate, and only after long separation, when they have lost consciousness of each other, will they accept a second mate. Such loyalty among animals is always a source of interest to man, and is in itself significant.

Once in India a man out hunting killed a bird, and saw, as it fell to the ground, that its mate flew down seeking after it; and when he came near to take his prey he found the mate dead beside it. So impressed was he by the sight of the lifeless body lying beside its slaughtered mate that he never again went shooting. Constancy never fails to impress by its beauty.

In testing gold we recognize the real gold by its enduring qualities. The real gold lasts; and what the human being calls divine in character is something that is enduring in its beauty, and thus different, distinct, and apart from the world which is ever-changing.

The value of the things of life lies in the worth that man attaches to them; of themselves they have no value. There is a time when toys are treasures; but the child who cries for a toy comes to an age when he gives it away. And at every step in a man's evolution the values of power and position and wealth change in his eyes. And so as he evolves there arises in him a spirit of renunciation which may be called the Spirit of God. Gradually he recognizes the real value of those fair and lovely qualities of the spirit that change not. In the ideal of monogamy, in the ideal of devotion to one alone, abides a recognition of loyalty and constancy as being the most valuable, as being the most divine attribute of man.

To the poet, to the artist, whatever be his art, to the idealist, the idea of the one beloved is part of his being. With selfless sincerity he is faithful to his vision of beauty; and every thought that tempts him from his loyalty is to him like going astray. No social law or moral teaching is needed to chain him to his beloved; his inward impulse keeps him to her.

It has been no uncommon thing to find in any age, in any country, cases where a bereaved mate has been unable to live on after the death of the beloved. Most often one sees the bereaved one of a true union living a dead life, suffering a long-drawn-out crucifixion, till death terminates the enforced separation. Among the Hindus, that most idealistic of races, marriage gives a sacred position to the wife, so that she is, ideally, entirely dependent upon her husband to fight every battle of life for her; and to them the thought that a wife could marry a second time seems intolerable. Such stories of fidelity become so honored among the Hindus as to make sati a custom, and it becomes usual for Hindu women to imitate in their own lives the stories of great devotion, and by dying on their husband's pyre to give thus the greatest proof of loyalty.

from *Rasa Shastra*

ATTITUDE

The following article by Roy Eugene Davis, well-known Western Yoga teacher and author, is uplifting for those of us struggling with the concept of brahmacharya, transmuting and redirecting the sexual force. In our experience, guilt about sex is the cause of a tremendous amount of unnecessary preoccupation.

SEXUAL EXPRESSION AND SPIRITUAL AWARENESS
BY ROY EUGENE DAVIS

People should know that sex has a spiritual basis. Life is expressing through all of us. We see in the radiance and healthful glow of people in love something good and altogether beautiful, even sacred. Loving people are healthy, their step elastic, their eyes bright, their magnetism contagious.

Every man of accomplishment has had the right woman in his life to reinforce his nature and balance his energies. A man is not complete without his feminine counterpart, and the reverse is also true. Even spiritual leaders who do not marry have their close female companions: consorts, disciples, friends, or confidantes. The sexual relationship does not always find expression on the physical level. Because of the subtle interchange of vital forces between people there can be a blending and a fulfilling between two people who are enjoying each other's company and who are in mental and emotional rapport.

Unfortunately, in the minds of countless people on the spiritual path there is the thought that sexual union is contrary to living the divine life and is, at best, a concession to human nature. In the Adam and Eve story, in the minds of many, there is the implied belief that sexual intercourse was the cause of the fall of man.

Here is the truth about the fall of man. Certain souls, conscious of their divine nature, because of allowing their feelings to dominate reason, became involved with the material worlds and lost their intuitive ability. Overidentification with externals causes man to forget his true condition; then guilt, shame, and general inner confusion result. Unfortunately, it has been the practice in our Western culture to refer to young people who have not yet had sexual experience as being pure or innocent, a direct implication that sexual knowledge and experience makes one impure. Normal, healthy people wonder, "How can such a beautiful and enriching experience be impure?" Yet, there lingers in the subconscious the false teaching of the ages—producing psychological complications and much human misery.

To my knowledge, speaking as I do as one who once lived as a monk, to the letter of the rule, and now as a realistic householder, I can find no evidence that lack of natural sexual experience in any way enhances spiritual awareness. I have known a few men who were celibate by choice and who were health-minded and successful in their ventures. They chose to direct all of their time and energy into their creative work and thus were able to transmute and redirect sexual energy for other purposes. They were not devoid of a natural sex urge by any means. Through willpower and intense concentration they sublimated the urge. In every instance, however, these men did have close nonphysical relationships with women (or a woman) who shared their dreams.

A disciple of Paramahansa Yogananda's, while trying to explain his strong attraction for the lady of his choice, implied that Master could not really understand or relate to the situation since Master was a monk, he did not have a strong sexual drive. My guru set the young man straight on the matter by confiding: "I have as strong an urge as any other man—the only difference between you and me is that I meditate and draw the energy up into the higher centers and then use it for creative work."

The male-female relationship is of vital importance even if the physical closeness is absent because there is an electrical interchange which takes place when understanding people share their lives. A physical relationship is not always possible or desired. Mere proximity is sufficient to allow positive and negative energies to co-mingle; this results in balance and fulfillment. Such a relationship softens a man's nature and gives confidence and support to the woman.

NEW AGE SPIRITUALITY AND SEXUAL SUBLIMATION
EXCERPT FROM A TALK BY PIR VILAYAT INAYAT KHAN

In the spiritual schools of the past, spirituality was always associated with celibacy. There is no doubt that if a man has a wife and children, he has to concentrate more energy toward making a living than if he is living celibate. The marriage relationship does tend to make people involved in very practical things, so that if people want to live a spiritual life it is sometimes very difficult to combine it with a domestic life. That's why celibacy has been taught in most of the schools in the past.

But in the New Age there is a change taking place. It is part of the women's liberation movement, because women can go out and work and contribute to the marriage relationship on an equal basis. This brings about a change in spiritual ideals, because now both man and woman have to cooperate together in their spiritual life, and in their sexual relationship, which is in some ways directed by their spiritual orientation. It certainly affects the sexual relationship, because I think that the spiritual life makes one very sensitive, so that everything has to be sublimated; everything that one does in life has to be beautiful. Now, the sex relationship is something that can tend to draw a person down to passion, yet it is something that can be sublimated, depending on one's whole attunement. In the case of a spiritual couple, the relationship itself is transformed, transmuted by their idealism.

The satisfaction of the body tends to draw consciousness to the earth plane, tends to go counter to what meditation does, which is to draw one up. On the other hand, giving satisfaction to one's partner tends to counter that tendency, and there is a fulfillment there. In fact, the only feeling that saves sex is giving instead of seeking satisfaction. Seeking to give even physical pleasure to the other person instead of seeking it for oneself is something that saves a relationship from becoming crass egotism, as it is in the case of a lot of people.

Sexual energy is a very strong energy, which has been held back so much in the past; in this time of liberation, we may speak more freely about it than before. In the East it has been spoken of a lot. It is the energy of the race, something superpersonal. The energy to maintain the continuity of the race is stronger than that of the individual. So it is a very strong thing, rooted right in the being, which has its secondary characteristics, like the voice or the hair, manliness or womanliness. It is a very deep thing.

This energy, of course, can be sublimated. Tantra is a great art, developed particularly in the East, which consists of sublimating this energy. Some people have more capacity than others, just as some people can stay in the sun longer than others. It is an energy that can be sublimated altogether, but if its sublimation brings about a feeling of being disgruntled, then it shouldn't be done, because its aim is being defeated anyway.

I think that when one is doing yoga and living in a cave and so on, one can live brahmacharya [celibate]. However, living this kind of absolute celibacy in the world goes counter to the very nature of things. It was self-imposed by people who for social reasons found that it was the only way, because if they lived in a family they wouldn't be able to fully devote themselves to the spiritual life. But we live in a different time now.

Tantra is a way of sublimating sexual energy, but one can throttle oneself to the point of smothering oneself. The same thing is true of meditation; concentrating too strongly with your will would bring about a conflict in your being. So I believe in a more natural way of meeting the problem. Inasmuch as one can sublimate, the more one can sublimate sexual energy, the better. One should certainly not allow sexuality to descend into passion, but to rise.

TRANSMUTING SEXUAL ENERGY

CELIBACY
BY HAZRAT INAYAT KHAN

In all ages celibacy has been a religious and mystical ideal, and for two principal reasons. The first is that although the soul born into the world is led further astray by every fresh experience in life, nevertheless it is sex passion that causes the greatest delusion of all. The myth of Adam and Eve illustrates this truth; for whether it was a means taken by God or by Satan, it was at the hands of Eve that Adam ate the forbidden fruit, and not through any direct command or prompting that he himself received. And since man's final goal is the attainment of spiritual life, his life here on earth having been all in vain if he fails to achieve it, every effort has been made by religion to draw him away from that passion of sex toward which he is led by nature, and thus away from the greatest peril that his soul can encounter on its earthly journey.

And then again, whilst every expression of life, speech, laughter, tears, robs man of some part of his fund of energy, it is sex passion that makes the greatest demand of all; and therefore the idea of celibacy was presented, so that man might the better preserve his energy to pursue with singleness of vision that final goal of spiritual attainment.

Losses such as dimness of reason, weakness of thought, loss of memory, despair, depression, result when the inner being of man is starved because energy has been expended, and because there is no knowledge or skill in strengthening and sustaining the inner existence. At every moment of life and with every breath, the human being gives out and takes in energy; and whenever he gives out more than he takes in, he draws death nearer. But if energy is denied an outlet, it can be raised and used to sustain the mind and the inner being. For this reason mystics have often practiced seclusion, silence, and other forms of abstinence, to preserve energy for the sustenance of the inner life; and they have found that celibacy was the most effectual means of all upon this path. "It is the spirit that quickeneth; the flesh profiteth nothing."

But man's life can never be complete without woman, and this is the error that lies at the root of the ideal of celibacy. Man's life is incomplete without woman, whether one considers his social or his political life; and this is no less true if one considers his religious and his spiritual life. Without the sympathy of Christ for Mary Magdalene, and the closeness of the friendship of Christ with Martha and her sister Mary, the beautiful pictures of the Master's life would be incomplete. Among the prophets of the Semitic races, from Abraham down through the ages, there was always a woman to complete the course of their holy lives; and the great Hindu teachers from Brahma to Krishna are glorified together with their consorts.

Religious man, wherever found and whatever teacher he followed, has nevertheless been prone to look at contact with woman with contempt, with the thought of there being something unholy in the passionate love of woman. Indeed it is a question whether the libertine has actually debased woman as much as the religious man, who believes that to hold himself aloof from any woman with contempt and to strangle his love within him will be for his own spiritual benefit. And is it possible to debase woman and the position of woman in the scheme of life without debasing man and the whole of life?

In the evolution of the ego there is undoubtedly a development toward celibacy, but at the same time this development carries an increasing regard for woman, and the whole plan of life. Oriental philosophy, in discussing the ego, distinguishes between the nafs-e-ammara and the nafs-e-lawwama. The former is the individual whose whole existence is on the surface, engaged in the satisfaction of his senses in eating, drinking, in amusements, and in sexual indulgence; and the nafs-e-lawwama is the individual whose physical greed is controlled by intelligence, to the extent of making him discriminate between his pleasures. The nafs-e-lawwama rejects those desires and enjoyments that fall below a certain standard of taste which his intelligence sets for him.

The nafs-e-mutmaina represents a third and higher stage of development, in which the senses are under the control of mind. In this stage of evolution a man is absorbed in some ideal, or devoted to the achievement of some object in life, outside of self—art, invention, trade, and so on—and directs his energies into one channel. In his sexual passion he may be compared with the deer that comes to drink from the pool of fresh water lying hidden in the depth of the forest, pure and untroubled, to be frightened away by the least flutter of reflected shade that disturbs or distracts his attention. For him passion only exists when he loves; he cannot feel passionate when he does not love. Here at last is found the admiration of woman, the beginning of love, and the real love. What do the nafs-e-ammara or lawwama know, who think of love as a pleasure?

The furthest stage in development is the nafs-e-salima, in which man's consciousness is removed to an abstract plane. In the heart of a man at this point of evolution, love is raised from admiration to worship; his love is part of his being, and his passion, which is never expressed except in the intensity of love, may be compared to the alighting of a bird on earth to pick up a grain of corn. This man lives on a higher plane of life, judging by different standards, though his inspiration springs from the common life of existence. Thinker, visionary, or man of action, he becomes unable to regard anything as common or unclean; although in his contemplation of the mystery of life, his devotion to the pursuit of truth, and his self-sacrifice to the cause of humanity, he may become gradually realized above any material object. Having reached this point he is truly justified if he should strike the path of celibacy.

from *Rasa Shastra*

SEX IN MARRIAGE SADHANA
EXCERPTED FROM *BETWEEN PLEASURE AND PAIN,*
BY DHARMASARA SATSANG

Sexual Energy: Its Relationship to Physical, Emotional, Mental, and Spiritual Health

Sexual energy is related to the human organism in the following way: According to Ayurvedic physiology the digested food essence (rasa) of the food we eat is transformed into the seven body constituents (dhatus) by an involved step-by-step transformation process. The digested food is successively converted into lymph, blood, tissue, fat, bone, marrow, sexual secretions, and an eighth constituent called ojas—subtle light energy. The entire eight-step process takes about a month. The ojas, the most refined essence of the sexual secretions, in turn permeates and nourishes every cell of the body. With an increase in ojas there is a marked increase in well-being at all levels. With a loss of ojas everything deteriorates. The development of every body constituent is directly influenced by the one preceding it. Therefore, if an excessive amount of sexual energy is lost (loss of sexual energy happens mainly through sexual activity) the production of ojas suffers and a general deterioration in health takes place.

This might come as somewhat of a surprise to many, but according to Ayurveda, if diet and health are sound, then there is an excess of sexual secretions produced each month to allow for one monthly intercourse without detriment to physical, mental, emotional, and spiritual well-being. The sexual secretions in man are known as bindu and in woman as rajah. While a woman does not discharge her sexual fluids during intercourse, her sexual energy is, however, lost in subtler forms during the sexual act. Thus, male and female are in the same situation regarding preservation of sexual energy.

Sexual Abstinence: The Path of the Renunciate

Westerners often read or hear about traditional spiritual approaches and without understanding their implications try to imitate them. The results are usually disastrous. Probably the most misunderstood concept is sexual abstinence (brahmacharya).

In traditional Hindu society, when men and women reach their twenties they choose one of the two spiritual paths according to their natures: the path of the householder or the path of the renunciate (sadhu). The householder's path involves marriage, family, and all the responsibilities that go along with family life. The path of the renunciate is a solitary one involving full-time yoga practices such as yoga postures, breathing exercises, and meditation. Sexual abstinence is an essential part of this path. The renunciate practices celibacy not out of self-denial but solely to conserve his/her sexual secretions. The practices of yoga ulitize the stored sexual secretions by converting them to ojas. The ojas is then channeled to the higher chakras [energy centers] in the head via yogic exercises and awakens the transcendental aspects of the mind.

Religious Hindus revere and support renunciates, regarding their work as the most important contribution that one can make to society. They eagerly provide renunciates with their basic physical necessities such as food and shelter.

Moderation in Sex: The Path of the Householder

For westerners brahmacharya (abstinence) is almost impossible, because of free association with the other sex. But a person can be enlightened without brahmacharya if sex is lived in a natural way. Don't mix the sadhu trip in this thing. People go crazy by reading books and trying to become hermits.

Baba Hari Dass

The renunciate's path is a viable way of life in India for those rare beings who are suited to it. But in the West the situation is quite different. Firstly, society will neither support nor accept wandering mendicants. Secondly, Western social life is pervaded by sex, which makes it difficult to lead a celibate life. Even if a person abstains from sex, he will still dissipate his sexual energy through social and casual contact with the opposite sex. Except in very, very rare cases, the householder's path is best suited to the needs of Westerners.

The householder's path is equally revered in Indian culture. Of course, householders are not expected to be celibate. Brahmacharya (which literally means "living the life of God," living in our natural state, free from anxiety) in marriage involves the harmonious blending of the couple's energies at all levels, including sex. Brahmacharya for householders does not mean sexual abstinence but sexual moderation.

It is not important to observe strict celibacy when you are married. Sex is not love, it is a part of love. It can be a kind of devotional love between husband and wife. Just as too much eating or not eating at all are both dangerous, in the same way too much sex or complete abstinence from sex are dangerous to a peaceful relationship. They are not good for health and sadhana.

Baba Hari Dass

Natural Sex

A natural sexual relationship is one of the most important ingredients of a successful spiritual marriage. But what is natural sex? If we accept Western theories then there is something wrong if you don't have sex every few days. According to yoga, however, this type of sex is excessive and can only lead to loss of vital energies and cause physical and mental breakdown and the deterioration of the marriage.

Sexual suppression, on the other hand, is no better. When couples submit themselves to a rigid model of sexual abstinence, they create greater tension, separation, and confusion. This is a far cry from true brahmacharya—natural harmonious living. Accordingly, it is of great importance that we learn to open ourselves to the sexual instinct, become friends with it, feel at ease with it. If we try to deny the sexual urge, if we recoil from it, we deny life itself. We choke the vital energies at their source. Smothering the sexual drive is not brahmacharya. Accepting sex is the first step to true brahmacharya.

When sex starts to fall into its natural role in marriage, it enriches and harmonizes the relationship at every level. It becomes an expression of devotion, a sacrament between man and woman, a union of Shiva and Shakti. As the sexual relationship becomes natural, the sexual energies are conserved rather than dissipated and find expression in many ways of communication, not only through intercourse. What becomes especially noticeable is the true heart bond which grows when sex ceases to be an obsession. Marriage becomes a true union.

Taking the Obsession out of Sex

While neither excessive sex nor repression is healthy, very few of us are detached enough from sexual gratification that we can just have sex once a month without creating tension in the relationship. What is more, yoga recognizes the strength of the sexual samskara [conditioning impressions] and does not encourage a couple to rigidly limit sexual activity in the beginning. It simply will not work. Yoga does, however, offer many effective ways to normalize the sexual urge. Here are some of the fundamental ones:

DIET

Moderation in diet and selection of balances (sattvic) foods such as grains, milk and milk products, beans, nuts, seasonal fruits and vegetables, etc.— foods which are nourishing and easily digested, and which maintain a balanced state of body and mind.

Avoiding excesses of stimulating (rajasic) foods such as onions, garlic, sharp spices, salt, etc.

Completely refraining from taking enervating (tamasic) foods such as meat, fish, or eggs (unless these foods are necessary to life because of severe environmental conditions).

HATHA YOGA AND MEDITATION

Regular Hatha Yoga practices such as the four purification exercises, yoga postures, breathing exercises, and regular meditation are very effective ways of transmuting the sexual energy. (See exercises for sexual transmutation, pages 70–79.)

MUTUAL LIMITATION OF SEX

While diet and the techniques of Hatha Yoga go a long way toward controlling the sexual impulse and redirecting the energy, they won't be fully effective unless there is *mutual agreement* to limit sexual activity. This requires much patience, tolerance, and compromise. It should be done gradually. In our experience a good approach is to initially limit sex to once a week, then three times a month, then twice, and eventually once a month. In time sexual activity will occur only when there is genuine need.

We have seen in the preceding section of this book that redirecting the sexual force is an essential aspect of spiritual development. In our practice we have found that the most middle-of-the-road methods for redirecting the sexual force into higher creativity and spirituality are the techniques of Hatha Yoga.

In the following section we therefore present the four classical purification techniques of Hatha Yoga. These are followed by several asanas, or postures, which are particularly effective for transmuting sexual energy into a higher expression.

THE FOUR PURIFICATIONS

In performing these exercises a person should be seated in a comfortable cross-legged position, with head, neck, and back in a straight line. They should be practiced on an *empty stomach,* at least two and one-half hours after eating. The four purifications should be done at least once a day and, if desired, up to four times a day. The best times to practice them are the first thing in the morning, midday, around sunset, and late at night.

I. Alternate Nostril Breathing without Breath Retention (Nadi-Shadan)

This exercise is designed to purify and balance the subtle and physical nervous systems and allow the life force to flow freely through the subtle channels. It makes the mind still and clear.

DESCRIPTION

1. Sit in any comfortable cross-legged position.
2. Put the thumb of the right hand on the right nostril and the last two fingers of the right hand on the left nostril. Open the left nostril and let all the air out through it.
3. Slowly breathe in through the left nostril until the lungs are full, making as little sound as possible. When breathing in, the diaphragm is raised slowly and the abdomen is kept flat.
4. After the in breath is completed, close the left nostril, lift the right thumb, and slowly exhale through the right nostril. When exhaling, gently push the navel inward.
5. Without a pause, inhale through the right nostril, as in number 3, and exhale through the left nostril, as in number 4. This is one round. Start with ten rounds and gradually increase to twenty-five rounds.

II. Skull Shining (Kapal Bhati)

This exercise is specifically designed to remove congestion in the nasal and bronchial areas. It also stimulates the organs of digestion and elimination; rids the body of excess carbon dioxide and replenishes it with an abundant supply of oxygen; and invigorates the entire nervous system.

DESCRIPTION

It consists of a series of rhythmic, rapid, shallow-breathing movements done from the navel area. Effort is applied only to the exhalation; the inhalation is passive.

1. Sit as for the first exercise.
2. Exhale by pushing the abdomen inward with a quick, piston-like stroke. As soon as the stroke is completed, the abdomen is relaxed and inhalation happens automatically. Repeat at the rate of one breath per second, and do between 50 and 100 repetitions.
3. After completing the rapid breathing, take a long, slow inhalation until the lungs are filled and concentrate on the space between the eyebrows (third eye) for a few seconds. Then exhale slowly. This is one round. Do up to two rounds of 50 to 100 rapid-breathing movements.

III. Fire Cleansing (Agni Sar Dhauti)

This exercise is designed to stimulate and strengthen the glands, organs, and chakras which are responsible for digestion and assimilation. Growth, strength, and resistance to disease depend on their proper functioning.

Fire cleansing, done correctly and regularly, eliminates impurities in the abdominal area; removes functional organic defects of the digestive system; and aids and strengthens the digestive "fires" by increasing and controlling the special life force necessary for digestion and assimilation.

DESCRIPTION:

1. This method can be practiced standing with the legs spread about a foot apart, knees slightly bent, and hands on the thighs, fingers turned inward. It can also be done sitting as in the preceding two methods, except that the hands are now placed on the knees, fingers turned inward.
2. Either way, first exhale all the air from the lungs and apply the chin lock if possible.
3. With the breath held out, vigorously draw the abdomen inward so that the navel is pulled toward the spine. Relax the abdomen and allow it to return to its normal position. Rapidly repeat this movement 20 to 100 times on a single expelled breath.
4. When it comes time to take another breath, stop pulling on the stomach and breathe in slowly. This completes one round. Do one or two rounds of 20 to 100 pulls.

IV. Anal Sphincter Contraction (Ashwini Mudra)

This exercise stimulates the subtle energy center at the base of the spine (muladhar chakra) and pushes life force to all parts of the body. It is also helpful in relieving hemorrhoids, constipation, and prostate problems.

DESCRIPTION:

1. Sit in any comfortable cross-legged position; even a squatting position will do.
2. Inhale slowly and retain. Lower the chin onto the chest.
3. While holding the breath, contract and relax the anus in quick succession. Do between 20 and 100 contractions on a single inhaled breath.
4. When it comes time to exhale, lift the chin slowly and breathe out gently. Do up to two rounds of 20 to 100 contractions.

YOGA POSTURES

Yoga postures are one of the most effective ways of insuring a healthy body. Their main purpose, however, is to convert sexual energy to subtle or spiritual energy. The following postures in particular are extremely useful in sublimating sexual energy.

1. Shoulderstand

DESCRIPTION

Lie on your back with legs outstretched. Slowly raise your legs to a position perpendicular to the ground. Next, support your lower back with your hands and push yourself erect so that your body is supported on your shoulders.

BREATH

Inhale while raising your body into the shoulderstand. Breathe normally while in the shoulderstand. Exhale while lowering your body to the ground.

TIME

Start with one-half minute and slowly increase to five minutes.

2. Headstand

DESCRIPTION

Sit on hands and knees. Interlace your fingers and form a tripod with hands
and elbows. Place the back of your head into the cupped hands and the top of
your head flush on the ground. Slowly raise your legs so that your body is
perpendicular to the ground.

BREATH

Inhale while going into the headstand. Breathe normally while in the
headstand. Exhale while lowering your body.

TIME

Start with fifteen seconds and slowly increase to five minutes.

3. Seated Forward Bend

DESCRIPTION

Lie on your back with hands by your sides. Slowly raise your upper body to a seated position. Keeping knees straight, bend forward and clasp ankles or feet.

BREATH

Inhale while raising your body to a seated position. Exhale while stretching forward. Breathe slowly while in the posture. Inhale as you come back up to a seated position and exhale as you bring your body back to the lying position.

TIME

Start with fifteen seconds and increase to one minute.

4. Cobra

DESCRIPTION

Lie on your stomach with hands placed underneath your shoulders. Slowly push your hands into the ground and extend your head and back, keeping thighs on the ground.

BREATH

Inhale as you extend backward. Breathe slowly while in the cobra position. Exhale as you lower your body.

TIME

Start with ten seconds and increase to thirty seconds.

5. Cowhead

DESCRIPTION

Bend the left knee and place the left foot by the side of your right hip. Cross the right leg over the left leg and place the right foot by the side of your left hip. Stretch the left hand up your back. Stretch the right hand over your right shoulder and clasp the left hand. Straighten your back. Repeat the cowhead position by reversing the leg and hand positions.

BREATH

Inhale while going into the cowhead position. Retain your breath while in the position. Exhale while releasing the posture.

TIME

Start with a five-second retention and increase to twenty seconds.

6. Duck

DESCRIPTION

Sit on your heels and place your hands on the ground in front of your feet with fingers pointing outward. Place elbows underneath your knees so that the weight of your body rests on hands, feet, and elbows. Lift your head up and raise your feet off the ground.

BREATH

Inhale while going into the duck pose. Retain your breath while in the posture. Exhale while releasing the posture.

TIME

Start with a five-second retention and increase to twenty seconds.

7. Head Foot

DESCRIPTION

Stand with legs separated three to four feet apart, and clasp hands behind your back. Bend your left knee and bring your head toward the left foot. Stand erect and repeat the posture to the right foot.

BREATH

Inhale while bending. Retain breath while in the posture. Exhale while returning to the upright position.

TIME

Start with a five-second retention and increase to twenty seconds.

SPIRITUAL MARRIAGE

Hazrat Ibrahim Khawwas, an eminent saint, relates that once he traveled to a certain village to visit an old man who was much reputed for his piety. When he went to the house of the old man he found that there were two prayer niches in different corners. In one sat the old man, in the other an old woman. Both of them were clean and bright, though frail on account of excessive devotion.

Hazrat Ibrahim stayed at the house for three days. At the time of departure, he asked the old man, "What relation to you is that chaste lady?" The old man answered that she was his wife.

Hazrat Ibrahim was somewhat surprised at this revelation, for during these three days the old man and woman had treated one another like strangers. The old man said that such had been their actual behavior for the last sixty years.

The saint felt inquisitive, and the old man told his tale: "We fell in love as children and wanted to marry, but her father refused. I felt unhappy for a long time, and prayed to win her. Then her father died, and her mother married her to me.

"On our wedding night, my bride said, 'What great happiness God has given us; let us in thanksgiving refrain tonight from passion of the body and worship God.' I agreed, and both of us prayed for the whole night. Next night she asked me to do the same. On the third night I said, 'Two nights we have given thanks at your suggestion; let us do the same tonight at my suggestion.' We prayed to God for all the night. And thereafter this process was repeated every night, sometimes at my suggestion, and sometimes at the suggestion of my wife, and this process has continued for the last sixty years."

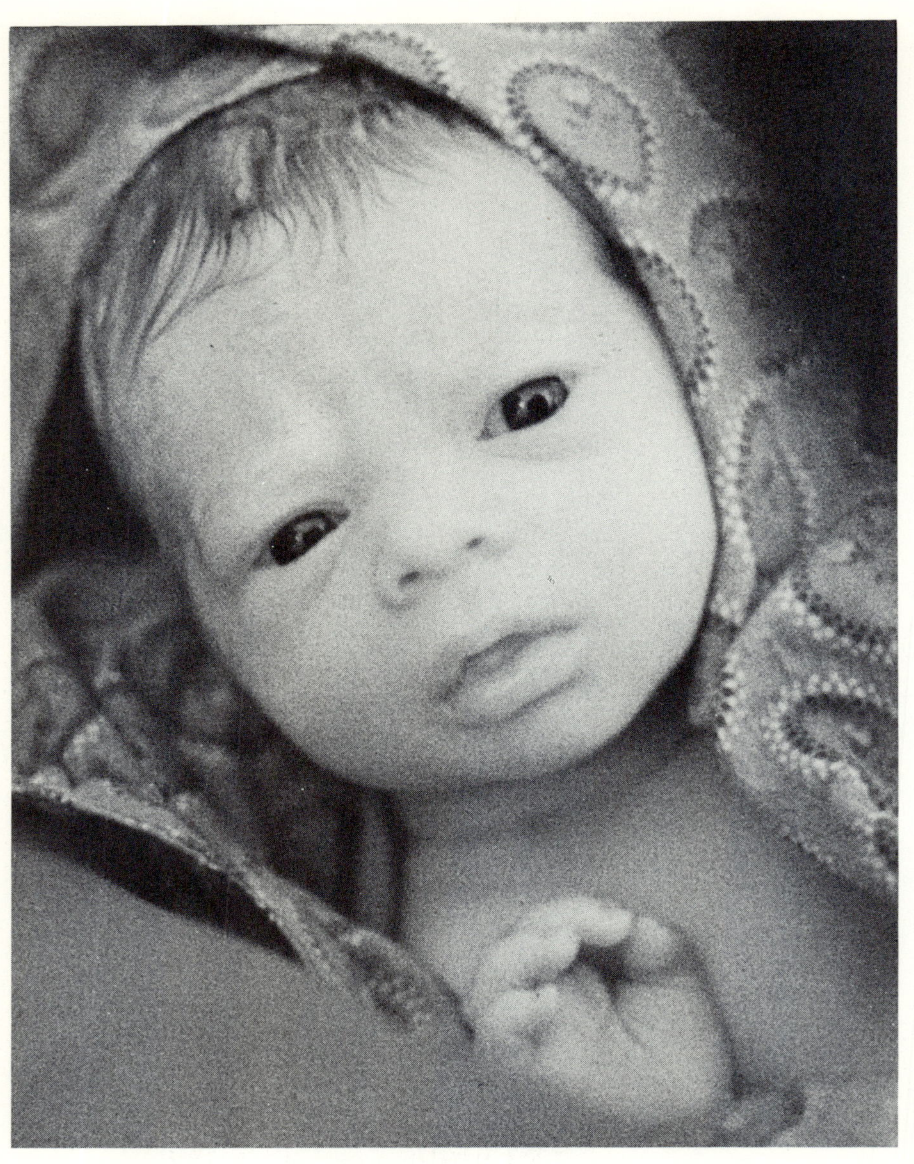

IV
PARENTHOOD AS A SPIRITUAL METHOD
(Sadhana)

A baby takes birth in the world by his own samskaras [conditioning impressions] and then the parents pass on their samskaras and their friends-relations-society-culture; all kinds of samskaras fill the baby. It's like filling an empty bag with all kinds of garbage—but the baby is able to empty the bag at any age in his life. Although it is also by his own samskaras "to get rid of that garbage."

A newborn baby is the purest form of a human being. This purity remains until the baby understands my-mine-you-yours.

Baba Hari Dass

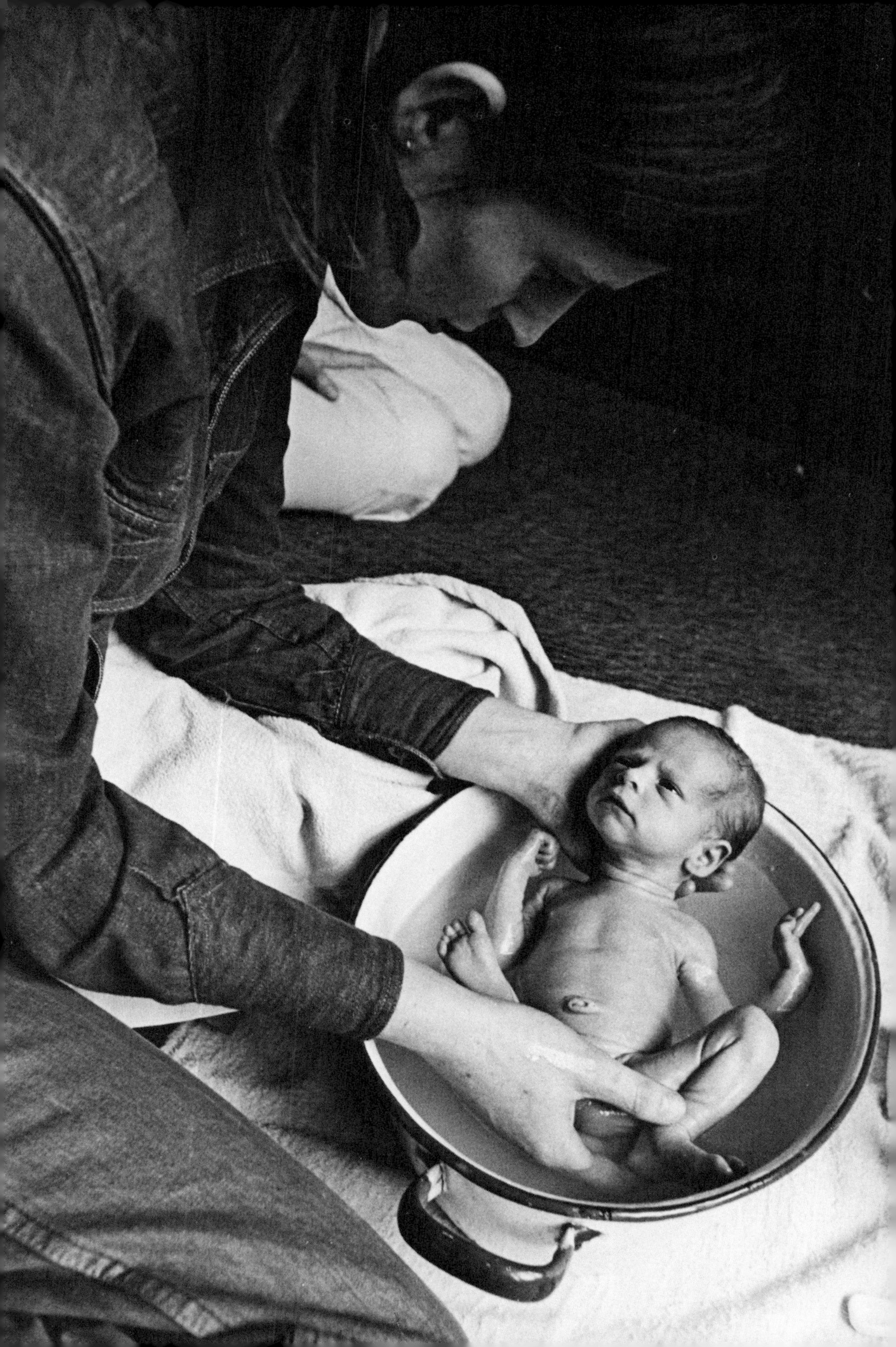

THE RELATIONSHIP OF MOTHER AND INFANT:
A NEW PERSPECTIVE
BY STEPHEN GASKIN

We have just been fortunate enough to meet Marshall Klaus. He's the president of Case Western Reserve University Medical School, and he's touring the United States from hospital to hospital right now with films that prove that newborn infants track and see and respond from birth. And he's proving it. And then beyond proving it, he's pointing out that infants are treated as if they were mummies or something. They are treated like sausages. He shows how aware they are; he shows that not only will they track when you hold your finger up, but when you talk to them they will dance to the rhythm of your words, moving perfectly in time with each syllable you make. With films. And he has slowed those films down so you can see in synchronicity with the words as they danced. It's the most mind-blowing thing. It's the most psychedelic thing I have ever seen on film in the strictest sense of the word "psychedelic." Because it is pure third eye. It isn't colors and trips like that; it is third eye. Real vision. It knocked me out.

And then the next thing that he's proving is that the mother and the baby having eye contact and being left alone together for the first hour makes a difference in child abuse and adoption, all that kind of stuff. He's proving that if you take the baby away from the mother, it keeps them from bonding. It's like mutual imprint. And it's so fast that you can take a baby lamb that's been with its mother for fifteen minutes and she'll always find him in a crowd and always know which one he is. And if you take a baby lamb that has been with his mother for ten minutes she might take him back or she might take another lamb back. If you take a lamb that's only been with the mother for five minutes, she will kill it in a matter of minutes.

What it comes down to is the state does not have the right to imprint the children. It's a basic right; it comes under the Ninth Amendment to the Constitution—"That certain rights have not been herein enumerated is not to be construed [as meaning] that there are not other rights that are not enumerated herein that are retained by the people." And this is one of them; it is really seriously important. The state does not have the right to imprint the children.

That's what Marshall Klaus' film did for me. It showed me that even when a kid is a newborn it responds to the reality feeling. I've said "hi" to a brand-new baby and it has said "hi" back to me. Just said "hi" right back to me. Just like when you drip a drop into a cup of milk. At first it goes down into it and a ripple happens. And the ripple does its thing and it causes the same size drop that went in to jump back up.

You understand why it works, but it's still a miracle.

The Talmud says that you are not permitted to become a teacher unless you become a father and a mother. That means when you really want to teach somebody you have to be on both levels; it has to be on the level of the father, and on the level of the mother, and always on the level of giving light; every word you utter has to be light. . . .

You know, when we have children, we invite them from high heaven. We say, "Children, please come to this world."

So, my baby comes. Then my baby asks me, "What did you bring me here for?"

And we say, "I want you to make money, I want you to watch the Late Show, I want you to have a good time, I want you to have fun."

No wonder they answer us, "For that, for that you have the chutzpa [the nerve] to bring me down from Heaven? What's going on here?"

God says to us, the Bible says, "Love your parents, honor your parents." Why doesn't it say "Love your children"? It's a little bit important. Maybe it's even more important for the parents to love children than for children to love parents.

You know, there are many people who wake up in the morning, and they are ready to jump and run to the synagogue and serve God—which is very sweet and holy. But it's not the highest. It is not the highest. Oblabita Vaditcha, one of our holy masters, would wake up in the morning and the first thing he would do, he would run down to the houses of children who had no parents. And he would say good morning to them. You know how deep this is? You know how children really need someone to say good morning to them. We adults need it also, but we pretend we don't need it. You need one person to say good morning to you, to really say good morning to you.

Children, their inside is absolutely untouched by anything. Some of us see that when you do a bit wrong, you become a bit wrong. The inside gets touched. But with children the inside is strong, beautiful, and holy. So when they wake up in the morning, you have to connect the inside to the outside. It is very important.

Listen to this, sweetest friends. There is a world of twoness and there is a world of oneness. Before God created the world, there was only One. When God created the world, it became two—God and the world. What we have to do—God made two and we have to make one again. We have to turn the world back or lift it up to make one again. It is up to us.

If you want to have children, then you have to study every day, husband and wife, the story of creation. If you want to create a new world, connect yourself to God's words when he created the World.

According to our tradition, the holiness of the baby depends on the closeness of husband and wife. It's as simple as that.

Reb Schlomo Carlebach

Even the word "children" is a relative fantasy. They are us in small bodies, seeds that are unfolding. In the same way that you provide a plant that you are cultivating the best possible environment for it to reach its full growth, you should provide children with the sort of environment that allows them to maximize their creativity and potential. The particular direction a seed takes is not determined by your goals; and neither is it with children. Instead of forming children to fit into our models of consciousness—to be "bright," athletic, or even "adjusted" in the psychological sense—you honor their being. You accept individual differences because you are not attached to the fact that one particular style is any better than any other. There is no subtle feeling that the person has failed.

We have got to develop an approach to education where parents and teachers are moving toward honoring the space of the child; keeping in mind that the best thing we can do to accomplish our overall social goals is to work on ourselves. All we can offer anyone else, including our own children, is our own being, our own particular level of evolution.

Whatever work we are involved in, parent or otherwise, our path is the same. It is to use the situation to become passionately aware, quieter inside, present in the moment. By working on ourselves, in this way, we begin to develop a very different view of education.

A better way of dealing with early childhood education would be to create a safe, supportive environment that would allow the child to stay close to his

or her direct and immediate experiences. We can well afford to allow our children to remain in a nonlinear, nonlogical space until such time as they can develop the tools of the intellect without emotional attachment to them. Our greatest predicament in this culture is our emotional attachment to the intellect. We have become hooked on it as a power tool. The idea of not using it even in periods of meditation is very difficult to take.

The insidious part of our reinforcement of intellectual development in schools is that we have been relying primarily on emotional conditioning and love. The teacher is under pressure to have the children succeed, so he or she develops a method that works in a subliminal or nonconceptual way. Love then becomes a system of control. We have been using emotional rewards and punishment to teach people to think in a linear-analytical and rational way.

We have to start providing more meditative spaces in our educational programming.

Ram Davis, "Toward a Higher Education," *East-West Journal,* September 1974

Children are our absolute final teachers, because they have our stuff 100 percent, and they are going to throw it back to us, call us on it, every time. And they are so psychically linked to us that you can be trying, and just as you try to get it together and really are straightening up and getting some things together, they are going to go right to the marrow of it and give you another job. And that's why they "drive us crazy." Because it is exactly the stuff we need to look at. And if you can get to laugh at that and start to realize that those kids are your mirrors, doing their utmost to get you completely clean. Because, again, it's so much like the male/female thing—they being the male energy and you being the female, receptive. When you get whole, you automatically make space for them to be whole. There is nothing to do to make your kids okay, healthy, and loving beings, except take care of yourself and get yourself cleaned up. Then you will automatically radiate the space. Because they're going to buy your reality.

Patricia Sun

Children at first try to test their parents or teachers. If they win then they don't obey, but if they accept that the parents or teachers are stronger, then they become very close.

Baba Hari Dass

SPIRITUALIZING THE HOME
BY SHARING WITH CHILDREN
BY GAYATRI DEVI

When our family met our spiritual teacher Sant Keshavadas, we were already practicing yoga and meditation. However, there was little we did together as a family in a spiritual way. Our daughter was then three years old and we felt that though she had been exposed to yoga, it was now time that some in-depth training should come her way.

We began by changing our thoughts about our home. We stopped thinking of it as just our house and began looking upon it more as a temple. Slowly I began to put up more pictures and little reminders that would help us remember the presence of God from minute to minute. We expanded the meditation corner into a meditation room. We had an altar built and our family temple grew and grew.

Daily tasks began to be viewed as spiritual duties. Dirty dishes became an integral part of our spiritual practice, housecleaning an opportunity to serve the Lord by making neat his temple. All the little, mundane household drudgeries took on a new meaning as we began to understand Karma Yoga.

For a family, ritual is really helpful. Because of the enormity of the work involved in family life, little time remains for lengthy meditations, hours of study or practices. However, many rituals and small bits of concentration can be done throughout the day. Ten minutes in the meditation room chanting and offering fruits and flowers to the Lord can be done quite easily and most enjoyably with a baby and small children. Japa [repetition of God's name] can be counted in mending stitches, or in shelling peas for the dinner table. Chanting to yourself and your children is a very good practice when driving the car. Much can be accomplished in this way simply by seizing the moments that go by unnoticed and transforming them.

Of course, the older religions have known this for ages! Religions are rich in daily rituals, most of which are performed in the home by the women and mothers of the household. It is the responsibility of the women in the families to see that the hearth fires of the daily practice of the presence of God never go out.

When we met our teacher we were taught how to perform the daily ceremony of worship to Lord Panduranga Krishna and Rukmini. This daily puja [devotion] involves many prayers invoking the Lord and feeding, bathing, and offering various things to him. It is a very personal and warm sort of ritual, bringing God very close to be spoken to and made friends with. These pujas can be done with children. I think it must be quite pleasing to children to see and hear their parents singing the prayers in the morning, or chanting to them as they fall asleep at night.

But even before we learned the formalized puja there was many a time we did pujas of our own. Sincerity of heart is what is important, and many were the times my daughter and I lit a candle, offered fruits and flowers, and bowed before our homemade altar. We composed our own types of prayers or borrowed the devotions of many religions.

To sustain the spiritual vibration of the family meditation room, the family must respect its existence. Therefore the children are not allowed to play in it. The area is kept secluded and quiet. Offerings of food are kept fresh and attractively arranged on the altar. Fixing the offerings is an activity both boys and girls enjoy. Eating the blessed food after it has been offered is even more enjoyable to them. I have found that to the innocent mind of a child nothing is more soothing or healing than the blessing bestowed in the form of sanctified food or water. Many an ailment or discomfort has been helped in our house by a piece of altar fruit or drink of puja water.

Children also enjoy making decorations for the family worship. Flower arrangements, strings of beads—both are tiny offerings that make the children feel they are part of things. They also enjoy the work of cleaning the meditation room. Dusting the photos and books and freshening up the place serve as ways to include the young in spiritual practice.

The importance of group participation needs to be stressed. Many families feel they can go on with each member doing their sadhana in private. Of course a certain amount of privacy is essential, but in a family situation too much is not good. Obviously our children have been born into yogic families for a reason. The *Bhagavad Gita* clearly states that one who had been on the spiritual path in a previous life will be reborn into a family that can aid his spiritual advancement. It is therefore our duty to educate and guide from birth, and even before, the returning souls entrusted to our care. Indeed, long before the actual birth of our children we should be invoking and praying a high soul be born in our midst. These things we should do for the betterment of humanity.

When our daughter got to be four years old, we began a "Sunday school" in our home. This was a big experiment as at the time there was little or nothing to use as materials for educating small children about God outside of the traditional Sunday school materials. Relying mainly on the ancient art of hari katha [Hindu storytelling] we took stories from the religious works of all times and places. We accompanied these with chants and songs; then knowing children's love for making things, we added work projects, art work, and games we had made up. I have kept a written record of these lesson plans to be used for my son when he becomes a little older and for any other children who are interested.

These simple little lessons which I type up for the children every week have afforded my daughter a very good beginning and a kind of platform to rest upon when confusing times come her way or she is assaulted by the usual growing pains we all go through growing up in American society. It has given me a satisfying feeling too, as I feel I am influencing her growing years in a positive way.

There are so many ways to glorify the daily round of householder life. It is a great test of one's own creativity. Another time-consuming event in the life of any family is meals and the time spent in preparing and eating food together. A home garden, no matter how small, can be a tremendous learning ground. The daily miracle of watching things grow from seed, then blossoming and eventually giving themselves to be consumed by us is a scripture in itself. The good that is derived when families work hard together on land is also priceless.

Everyone knows the importance of cooking consciously. It is a lot of fun to teach a son or daughter how to do this, too. Even the smallest children can learn what is good for them and why. A favorite game of ours is identifying the various beans and seeds on the kitchen shelves and then concocting new ways of using them.

The kitchen can be a wonderful temple of childlike sadhana. Cooking is such a cosmic process. Products of the earth mingle with the elements of pure water and, combined by the warmth of fire, another mysterious element, result in a wonderful gift from God to be offered again to God and eaten by God's children. It can be a source of many fine lessons, the kitchen.

Most families pray before eating. We decided to expand the normal dinnertime prayers and add some meditation and reading from the various holy books of all religions. We started with the Psalms, added Tulsidas' *Petition to Ram,* and since then have opened the doors on the great religious works of the world and their many-hued but unified messages.

Of primary importance to spiritual families are the many holy days which can be celebrated throughout the year. Our family, being more universal in its outlook, was unable to be partial to the celebrations of any one religion. My husband had been raised with the beauties of the Jewish year and I was unwilling to part with Christmas, and our teacher had introduced us to a host of new and sweet celebrations. We decided to celebrate them all, including revising and writing a few new ones.

We are fortunate enough to live in the country. We also live in a northern climate where the seasons pass by in a dramatic fashion. So many of the religious observances of the world involve a particular season or time in the natural cycle. Easter's resurrection, for example, comes just at a time when the earth is being released from its prison of winter ice. It seems right that these celebrations should correspond somehow with nature as this earth too resides within the body of God and is part of the Cosmic Being.

Naturally, we had to alter slightly some of the actual practices of these holiday celebrations to adapt them to our particular way of life. At first we wondered if it was all right to tamper with the strict observances of various religions. However, we felt that as long as we did so with the utmost care and attention to the inner meanings of these holy days, such a thing would be all right. For example, being vegetarians, we had to slightly rearrange the Seder dinner on Passover. Therefore, we took the symbolic meaning of the particular food and substituted it with something else. We substituted fruits and flowers for the traditional offering of a roasted lamb bone. We emphasized the idea of Passover as being the celebration of the special protection and love God bestows on those who follow His commandments and the freedom that can be found by trust in God and surrender to Him. We accompanied this with many wonderful Bible stories and readings from the Psalms.

At Christmas we bedecked the trees with the symbols of the religions of the world. We talked and read much about the birth of great avatars [incarnations of God] and saints and their particular roles in the world.

When one remembers childhood, the holidays stand out in one's mind. They are molding events, special days that leave lasting impressions. They can be used to teach our children about all faiths and peoples and the truth of the Vedic statement, "Truth is one, many are the ways."

Holy days can be used, therefore, to show the many aspects of the one God. They can show the beauty of the Holy Family, or tell a story of deliverance and sacrifice, forgiveness and fasting. Each holy day leaves a subtle impression on the young mind, which then can grow up with the knowledge that God is all, creative, preservative, destructive; that there is a time for feasting, a time for fasting; and that all these dualities have their origin in Oneness.

We can use celebrations as an excuse to include one another in an expanded family feeling. Invite your friends and neighbors to add their particular contributions. Love expands this way. And with it, so do we.

To spiritualize a home is to spiritualize daily existence. The secret of doing it is to seize the moments that go by unnoticed to experiment and develop one's own sense of time. Moments can slip into hours being counted by mantra [verbal expressions of oneness], and lives go by in prayer and song.

Many people lament their lives as householders. It is not without its obvious drawbacks. However, time is there for us to take and mold as we see fit. The yogi has the power to hold world order in his hands; if dharma can prevail in the home where the next and succeeding generations are growing, then there is hope that this world will see better times.

It is taught that this world is God's lila, His sport, His play. If so, then let us seek to play to the utmost of our ability, remembering who is the audience and that all the other actors are but reflections of the One Divine. Let us, therefore, play along with Him. Play with our children, our partners, our homes, and our passing lives so that we may lay our days before His feet, satisfied that we did our best.

It is never too soon in the life of a child for it to receive education. The soul of an infant is like a photographic plate which has never been exposed before, and whatever impression falls on that photographic plate covers it; no other impressions which come afterwards have the same effect. Therefore, when the parents or guardians lose the opportunity of impressing an infant in its early childhood, they lose the greatest opportunity.

To raise an infant, to look after it, to educate it, and to give oneself to its service is as much and as good as the work of an adept, because an adept forgets himself in meditation and a mother forgets herself by giving her life to the child.

Hazrat Inayat Khan

Blessed be the mother who gives to her child the tools with which to cut through the negativity of this world, through to the self within. Very often one of these tools takes the form of the loving embrace of the mother's own body—the warmth, the pulse, the gentle words, the aura within which the child loses him/herself for a few moments of comfort. The ability to love and be loved by another is a valuable tool.

But there are times when even this is not sufficient, times when the soul must find its own calm. The mother can best intuit these times, and a useful tool to provide the child with is the technique of "wrapping" and solitude.

We use a blanket or towel and wrap the child lovingly, with arms straight at the sides. The wrap should be firm enough so that the child cannot wriggle out of it. Then, while chanting, or singing, or with gentle words, rock the child back and forth on the back. If the child is on its stomach, then gently massage the spine. Then leave the child's aura.

Wrapping should never be done if the parent has any hint of anger or frustration. It is nice to create an atmosphere conducive to relaxation, i.e., candlelight, incense, comforting music.

The child may push strongly for a few minutes (it is more fulfilling to them to have something to push against than to flay their arms and legs furiously), and then enter into a peaceful state of relaxation and calm. This strengthens the nervous system and *instead* of exhausting themselves from crying, and putting themselves to sleep out of exhaustion, wrapping allows them to channel their nervous energy into the stuff of ecstasy.

When I first went to use this technique on my three-week-old girl, I was still very apprehensive of it. It seemed repressive. But when I saw her crying turn into a state of ecstasy within a few minutes, I was thoroughly convinced. It is a beautiful thing to watch. I continued until she was one year old.

I hope you can use it.

Guru Raj Kaur

There is an overwhelming tendency in our society to discredit anything which is unpleasant or uncomfortable. Old people and sick people are shut away and millions of dollars are spent on pills to disguise pain. This tendency is reflected within our spiritual subculture's assessment of "godliness" or "highness." Thus a "high" woman will not feel pain in childbirth and a

"godly" parent will produce a saintly child. In reality, childbirth is letting oneself go (one must let oneself go) into the what-is, and one discovers there not only is ecstasy as one expected, but pain too. And that's all right. Likewise, children born into the most godly homes will manifest unpleasant qualities. The real eye-opener is when one realizes that it's still true to say, "All children are Buddhas."

Each parent is different and it's a distinct aspect of the sadhana of parenthood to find the midpoint for oneself and center oneself there, where neither the child, the parent or the universe is ripped off.

"Raising" a child is like a continuous act of healing. There's an almost constant output of energy demanded from oneself to another being. If the parent balks, as all parents do, at being the perpetual vehicle for the universe's nurturing energy, he frustrates himself and makes his job harder. If, on the other hand, the parent gives generously and without resistance to satisfy the child's real needs, his energy seems constantly replenished.

The New Age is replete with paradox. Nowhere is it more true than in parenthood that "the servant is the master."

Diana Nisson

The child does not strive, nor work, for he is still too weak for the labors which are to be his future tasks. All the same, he is already a person, for he eats the fruit of his first deed, a deed which sustains his whole life. What is his first deed? The drawing of nourishment from his mother. His food no longer comes to him of itself. He needs to draw nourishment in order to live. For this is the entire life of man, to strive is man born.

What name shall we give to the first "book of education"? Let us call it "The Chapter of Overflowing Love." Who teaches the first chapter? The mother. The beginning of all good comes from the mother. A child's education is begun by his mother. The mother who bore the child is the first to educate him, and the first lesson she teaches him is that of love.

This is the secret of education. When a person begins to strive, immediately an overflowing of blessing is opened for him. His striving is not for nought. When a person turns to his source and seeks to draw nourishment from his own well-stream, the latter opens for him and yields all its treasures to him. He seeks nourishment for the hour, but obtains nourishment also for the remainder of all his days. Such is the nourishment which a mother's love gives to her children. And in all the world, no love is greater.

A. E. Kitov, *The Jew and His Home* (reprinted with permission of Shengold Publishers, Inc., New York)

V

THE FAMILY: Interviews with Parents

Bringing up children is a very sacred undertaking and to many of us the yoga of parenthood is our most relevant sadhana.

SADHANA AND CHILDREN
EXCERPT FROM *BETWEEN PLEASURE AND PAIN,*
BY DHARMASARA SATSANG

M: Becoming a family of three is really a very different thing than just being a couple. Your whole life is changed in a way you couldn't possibly imagine—you get turned inside out and you get no sleep at first and anything you want to do for yourself cannot possibly happen. Especially for the mother. It's as if you have committed yourself to being the servant of a master—look after all his worldly needs, take care of him, carry his water pot—it's sort of like that except that it goes on day and night.

RD: It becomes a full-blown sadhana to serve your children.

G: A mother has the instinct to surrender to her children and to serve them completely. The vibration between the mother and her child is very full.

M: I was with our children all day today, and I got uptight so many times, I couldn't believe it. It's very hard, because I just don't want to surrender. I don't want to go on their trips and I don't want to focus on them as much as the situation requires.

RD: For me, too, I have my own things I want to be into, like I'll be writing or something and Manju will say "feed me" or "play with me"—what I see so much when I am with her is my inability to just be with her fully—my own trips are still more important to me. What happened with us a few days ago was, we were with Babaji, all three of us, and Manju started going through a trip. My first tendency was to try to cut her off—I mean, we were with Babaji—but I noticed the tendency and asked Babaji what to do in a situation like this. He didn't say anything, but found a book with a lot of pictures in it. He then took Manju on his knee and began to pretend to read to her, with a lot of humor and good vibe energy. He would point to pictures and pretty soon Manju was totally involved with him, pointing at the pictures he was pointing at, laughing and giggling. When they came to the end of the book, he put her back down on the bed and she was quite content to just be one of us. Quite a lesson. One of the biggest problems for me is that I have a lot of things in my head about what's important. Like, "I have to chop wood," or "I have to finish a chapter," "I don't want to be a babysitter." I'm learning through the grace of Manju's presence in our family how much my head has dictated what's important in a given moment and what's not. What I'm learning is surrender to what is. I'm seeing more how my tendency is to avoid surrendering to the situation, even though on one level it's true that the roof does need fixing, the firewood needs chopping, etc.

AD: Another avoidance can be not disciplining a child when discipline may be the appropriate action.

B: In working with the children at the nursery I've learned a lot about relating to children. One child, for example, is very demanding. The only way she knows how to get attention is by bringing out negative feelings; so we've learned that if we constantly plug into that when she's doing her trip we're reinforcing that in her. What I have to be conscious of is that when she's not putting out any negativity, to go over and hang out with her, because otherwise she just keeps getting her negativity reinforced.

RD: What do you do when she's being negative and demanding?

B: I let her work it out. I always tell her that I would much rather have her tell me what she wants. I recognize that when she's doing this a lot, she wants something from me, I say to her: "Kathy, I'd much rather have you tell me what you want; it really makes it hard for me when you're being mad," and she hears what I say.

RD: I think one more important aspect about this is the tendency to react. The first tendency when someone goes on a bummer is to put them down, to get angry, to react in some way. Sadhana teaches a person to stay calm, not to react.

B: It's a lot like marriage. I know that when I'm with another person, if I start getting angry, judgmental, etc., then something is being shown up inside me—one of my samskaras [conditioning impressions]. Children are incredible mirrors, because when they get to you, and they usually do, they're reflecting some of your attachments.

RD: At times, when I'm clear in my relationship with Manju, I can simply see that she's on a trip and not get sucked into reinforcing who she thinks she is at that moment. But this is extremely difficult for parents—to be clear and dispassionate with their own children. It's far easier to see someone else's kid's trip than it is to see your own kid's thing.

A: One reason why sadhana is so important is that if you're clearing your own stuff away from day to day and even moment to moment, you're not going to be as involved in reinforcing negative qualities in your own child, and those around you.

M: This is one reason why I like to use the term "guardian" instead of "parent." Simply remembering this at times helps me to not be so attached to the dramas of family life, allows me to get some leverage

over my own attachments, and to give to the situation what it really requires, rather than my own ego-investment.

RD: It is our duty and responsiblity to stop a child from running into the street, to tell a child about hot and cold, but, at the same time, a child has to find out about hot and cold by himself.

A: True, but one of the difficulties in this is that we have to treat a child as a child and not as an adult equal. There's always a lot of talk about that being the way to treat a child, you know, that a child should be treated as an equal. I think this means honoring the spirit of the child equally as one's own spirit, but digging at the same time that they are children. You are in the role of guardian to a soul in the role of child. They need guidance and attention as children, the kind of attention you don't give an adult. Children need to be protected and guided where they don't have the capacity to fully do it for themselves.

B: I think also that children need a certain form of security. We all do. That's why we need to give a child of two as much of an environment that he is able to relate to as possible—that's one of the responsibilities we have that is not so easy to tune into.

RD: Also, we have to guard ourselves from laying on them our models or ideas about what they need. One very obvious example of this is when parents are on a very specialized food trip and lay it on their kids. The children get very neurotic behind it. It's a clear example of the blind leading the blind, because the parents don't even understand their own nutritional needs. At the same time the kid may well begin to show his parents their attachment to their food trip. Suddenly it becomes the child's obsession to demand the very stuff the parents are dead set against. They want lots of milk or candy or bread or whatever, and they begin to test their parents like crazy.

A: I don't think it's exactly testing. I don't think they consciously try to push your buttons—they explore, they look for boundaries.

M: At a certain age, though, children can be adepts at pushing your buttons; they can pick up on a particular vibration quite easily. One time a kid came up to me and just out of the blue blurted out, "Look, I've got sugar!" One of the biggest things I have is wanting the kids to eat good stuff.

RD: In a situation where you may notice that a child's parents are on some sort of trip—like they may be laying something on their kid, and yours, if the two play together—then what do you do? I think it is one's duty to be straight about what one is seeing, but being sensitive to the right moment to say it and, above all, not being uptight.

AD: If a parent, or anyone for that matter, is committing an error it is necessary to tell them, but without aggravating the situation.

G: But there is a very fine line in mother-child attachment, which one has to be extremely sensitive to.

A: Somebody can tell me something about my relationship with Manju and if it's said without judgment, then I can really hear them. I can accept it without reacting. But if someone is judging me, then I can't accept what they're saying because I feel attacked. I just close up. I think the important thing to realize in relating to others, in terms of the mistakes they may be making, especially with parents, is to discuss your feelings without anger.

ON WHEN A COUPLE BECOMES A FAMILY
EXCERPT FROM AN INTERVIEW
WITH BARRY AND JOYCE VISSELL

RD: I meant to ask you, how has your daughter's birth affected your relationship?

J: While I was pregnant I was concerned about the effect the new baby would have on our relationship. I had seen many couples separating after they had children. I had been with Barry for eleven years when we became pregnant, and I didn't in any way want our baby to separate us. Now in counseling pregnant women I find that many of them have this fear. While pregnant I was able, as many women are, to establish a sort of communication with the soul of our baby. Whenever I would worry about the baby's effect on our relationship, there was always a loving response that she is drawn to us because of our love and will bring us even closer. It wasn't until after Rami came that I felt how true that is. Barry and I are much closer as a result of Rami, and she seems to have really accelerated our love for each other and for God. It was so important for me always to remember that Rami was drawn to us because of our love for each other, and that she doesn't want me to get so wrapped up in her alone that I forget Barry. This can happen so subtly, especially in the first few months, and women should be very alert for this. We have seen many men leave during this period.

B: When Rami first came, Joyce and I were both struck by the great responsibility. Joyce had an easier time with it as it was more natural and instinctive for her as a mother. For me, and for so many men, acceptance came much slower. I found myself making reasons to do extra errands and seeing more people in counseling in those early weeks. Finally, I felt how the responsibility of Rami is not to be accepted as a weight on my shoulders, but as a divine privilege. The more I entered into sharing the responsibility of her care, the more free I felt. This, of course, freed Joyce to be able to give more to both of us. I had this thing about the raising of a child being less important than my other work, but I give thanks that now I'm beginning to see I can do no higher service for the world in whatever I do, if I do it to serve God.

RD: I noticed you nursing your daughter, and this reminded me that Babaji once pointed out something to Aparna about nursing and potential separation from one's husband. She had nursed Manju for two and a half years, which he said was the perfect length of time. We were going through a whole sexual thing where Aparna didn't want to have sex for about two and a half years, and Babaji said, "Well, you're having sex with Manju all the time. Nursing her, that is sex. It fulfills the sexual need in women so that they may not relate as strongly on a sexual level to their mates." So I wondered where that was at for you guys?

B: It's been very far out, because in all the time Joyce and I have been together, thirteen years, I have never been given the opportunity to work as hard with my sexual desires. Joyce, with the nursing now, has hardly any desire for sex. So at first it was tough, for me especially, but also for Joyce. And we see this with all the couples we work with, children or not. The sexual relationship seems to be more important to the man as a way to express his tenderness and love, me included. But women are more naturally able to raise the energy to the heart center, expressing love more purely.

Most of the couples and individuals who come to work with us are on some spiritual path, formally or not, and so there usually is some awareness that eventually the sexual desire has to be transmuted. But what a great mistake to cut it off prematurely by the power of the human will, as so many are doing. So time after time a man, usually, will come in and announce, "Now I'm celibate," and the sexual desire has been so suppressed that I can almost see it coming out of his ears. If you practice feeling the presence of God, then the sexual desire becomes the desire to feel and express Divine Love.

That's what helped me tremendously. As long as I was feeling love for Joyce, as long as I held my attention on "How can I give to her?" rather than "What can I get?" I felt no desire to physically express it through sex. So many men haven't gotten that message yet, but I know they will. They just assume that when they feel love, the best way of expressing it is in bed. It's a habit carried through lifetime after lifetime. And you begin to understand that it has to be very deep. It's dealing with the forces of life itself . . . but misdirected to satisfy the sense desires, rather than for procreation, as was originally intended.

The beautiful thing is that as soon as the negative effects of sexual activity are felt, it then becomes a much easier matter to do something about it. With Joyce and me, because of nursing and her decreased sex desire, the frequency of our having sex diminished. During the intervals, we became aware of a momentum being built, a growing clearness and harmony in our relationship. Then I would start to give in to sexual feelings and thoughts, and feel that I needed sex and couldn't go any longer. Well, we started noticing after every sexual experience, however beautiful, a definite loss. A loss of energy, a loss of love and harmony, a loss of clarity of awareness. And it's getting more and more acute now. We feel now the falling away of sex desire, and it's happening fast. The love and peace we experience from meditation is vastly more beautiful than the peak moments of sex ever were.

SOCIAL YOGA
EXCERPT FROM AN INTERVIEW WITH PHILIP AND ELLEN, FROM THE FARM

RD: You told me about maybe thirty people and eighteen children living together in a house. Can you tell me how big this house would be, how many rooms it has? Our kids, I know, are super high energy, and I am sure yours are too. I'm interested in how you all live together in such cramped quarters.

P: The size of our household varies. At this point, I think we still have eight or nine of our caravan buses left. There was a time when we all just lived in those buses, until we built some houses and got set up. So we have been gradually moving into housing. Some of it is temporary housing. Our house, for instance, is what we call a tent house. It is hard to house a thousand people all at once. So we have had to do it in stages; the tent house we are living in has a foundation, a floor, walls, and a tent for the roof.

The size of our place is something like 36' by 40'. It has maybe eight or nine bedrooms, a living room, a kitchen—all the bedrooms off to the side for each couple.

What we have really tried to do in our house is to make a general living area, while keeping a place for each family. Very often parents will have their kids in a room next to theirs. I just can't see packing all the kids into a dormitory. I think that their relationship with their parents is too valuable to mess with. We have tried to respect each other's families at that level—aside from the help they may need from an interested friend—as far as advice and helping them raise their kids and whatnot are concerned.

E: The ladies in our household have an agreement because we're such close friends that if we see somebody's kid ripping his mother off, we say, "He's ripping you off, you know." And in-flight instructions on how to get it back together.

P: Usually it's more effective for the mother to do it herself, or the father, with their own kids.

E: They should. I don't think anybody other than the biological mother or the father, in some cases, should straighten the child out or discipline him in any way that's heavy karma. And we really emphasize that a lot—that the mother is in charge. Mother and father. I go to Philip when things get beyond my control.

P: It's interesting, because the kids are usually harder on their own mothers and fathers than they are on anybody else.

E: You have better vision about somebody else's kids because you are more objective and you can see what is happening. And that's how a cooperative living situation can really help. We all pool our resources and our vision in helping each other get smart.

RD: In the old days, in places like India or China, the whole family would live in one house, and all the children of all the generations would live together and really get along with and respect each other.

P: Well, wherever that is possible, it happens on The Farm. We encourage our parents or grandparents to come live on The Farm when they retire and that sort of thing.

RD: Are there any cases where parents of people on The Farm, who are not people on The Farm, are living there? And where there's a third generation, too?

P: Yeah. The father of someone living in our house has moved to The Farm. We have also had parents buying land right next to The Farm that we farm, and their plan is to build their retirement house on that property, so they can live near us and still have their own set-up.

RD: Can you tell me a story or example of how you actually deal with your kids?

P: The heaviest thing that you might have to do with a kid is to spank his butt. There are times when that may be necessary. The only thing about that, and Stephen emphasizes this frequently, is that you not be angry when you do it. If you are, then it teaches the kid anger; it doesn't help him at all.

E: Then they think you are the Nazis.

P: You have to have a really strong, loving relationship with your kids while still maintaining your parental position.

E: And the way you do that with your kid is to have him work along with you. That's really how we get a handle on our kids. As you say, your

kids have a lot of energy. Living in a big household situation like this can really rev up the kids at times. We have an agreement in our house that we've got to get the kids together first. We have one lady that just does the kids at suppertime—feeds the kids, makes sure they are covered. Because the kids are going to require a certain amount of attention. And if you don't give it to them, they'll rip you off for it.

P: They'll get it one way or another. If they can't get it another way, they start freaking out. I think that as far as discipline is concerned, also, you have to be really consistent, and when you tell a kid something once it ought to be sufficient. And then when the kids are together, that should be reinforced. You want to let the kids know that you are fair. You should be really fair; a kid will know if you're not.

E: Stephen says that a kid can smell a hypocrite a mile away. They have a really intuitive thing about fairness. But one thing I want to emphasize about the kids is about that energy, that really strong energy that they have. If you can find a way to channel that energy . . . like with our girls—it may take more time to do it this way, but it really works out in the end. If you're getting supper together, or getting your house together in the morning—just fit the kids into that schedule with something to do. You may get less done but you give them a sense that they are really taking part. Give them something real to do. Ina May mentioned that down in Guatemala she got some good relativity on how to raise kids. Because the kids are with their parents all the time, and it is such a heavy trip to live in a country like that where all the kids have to participate in the household and help out. They have to, just to survive.

RD: At what age would you say you could start, in your experience?

E: My three-and-a-half-year-old girl helps me wash dishes. She just loves it. And it's a trip to have her do it. If I just take the time to integrate her, she grows up and she's more stoned and she's grateful, and she loves me for taking the time to treat her like she's a person. And that is a really heavy thing. What we do is try to integrate the kids into everything we are doing, so we don't create a separate thing for them. Like they are over there playing in a corner, and we are over here doing our trip, putting out the "I don't have time, I don't have time" syndrome.

P: That's the best way to alienate your kids—you have your trip and they have theirs.

RD: What about, for example, when both of you have responsibilities in the community at the same time?

P: Well, that's something we are working out. In our case we are building something from scratch—this community is just a fledgling thing, five and a half years old. There's a lot to do, and it could very easily be a

full-time project just to keep up with our own work. And it's something that we are working out at the community level, too—keeping our school covered for people, maintaining the school building itself, etc. You need a lot of cooperation from the parents to keep your school going.

E: We have the school and we have babysitting groups. We have five ladies in the group who are really tight, who I have a good agreement with. Four days of the week I leave my three-and-a-half-year-old from around 10:00 to 5:00, and then I pick her up. And I take a day during the week to stay with their kids. That whole day I devote to the kids and babysitting, and the day they do it they devote the whole day. So it's an intensive day when you do it.

P: We are also building day care centers similar to those in China, where the community takes care of the community's children during the day; it frees up a lot of your work force.

RD: You have talked about how you deal with the kids within the household, but what about the kids' place in the community as a whole? The

Farm as a community can easily be seen as being something cut off from the rest of society, because it's really a very different experiment. How are the kids educated in terms of The Farm?

P: Well, I do know what you mean, and I feel that it is only fair to expose the kids to as much of the broader picture of society as we can. We don't want to isolate our kids any more than we want to be isolated. Part of it is that we are not isolated ourselves, and we have our kids participate with us in our interaction with the neighboring community. And we take them when we go to town, to Nashville and that sort of thing. We're trying to raise the kids with a really broad world view, so they are getting as much exposure to society and to the same kinds of cultural experiences that we have all had ourselves.

RD: Do they have any sense, as children, of being different from other kids because they live differently from other kids?

P: One of our kids, the oldest boy, stayed with my parents over a two- or three-week period this past summer, and he got a lot of flak about long hair to the point where he wanted his hair cut. He thought he looked like a girl and he didn't like that. But as soon as he got back to The Farm he relaxed, because all the other kids looked like he did.

E: We try to make an effort to educate the kids about this community. Our school has taken them on a tour of a fire station; they go to a swimming pool in a nearby town once a week and all the neighborhood kids are there. They have a lot of opportunity to interact with those kids and to work it out. That has been valuable.

RD: How do the other kids see them?

P: The other kids accept them pretty well. We've been here for a while, and after the first contact I think things improved steadily because they were able to see that our kids aren't different from them, and our kids could feel the same about them. There's really not any difference. Our schooling situation is a little different in some details.

RD: Can you give me some examples? Things that are emphasized?

P: In our school here? Well, first of all, we have an apprentice system. After a certain age, a certain grade, the kids start to . . .

RD: What grade?

P: Grade 5 or 6.

RD: Do you have grades 1 to 12?

P: Right. We had four graduating high school students last year. We will have a total of thirty or forty high school students this year. That's one of the fastest growing parts of our population. The teenagers are really getting amazing.

RD: Do they form a clique?

P: Well, the teenagers, a lot of them, live in the same place. It's what we call the Adobe. It's just a large apartment-house-type set-up that they built themselves.

RD: So what I'm hearing you saying over and over again is that the kids' energies are being channeled into the community?

P: Right. I think that the most important thing, especially for the teenagers, is that they not feel separate or alienated from the activity of the community.

RD: Are these kids who have just come to The Farm by themselves?

P: Some of them are runaways, some from detention homes. What we do about runaways is we contact their parents immediately—which very often the kids don't want to do. But we talk to them and explain that we would like to be a mediator between them and their parents, and that maybe we could be a kind of gearshift and help. We've had kids come with their parents hot on their heels. I remember one scene in the Gatehouse when a girl from Detroit came down to The Farm and her parents came the next day. We had this very emotional meeting at the Gatehouse—the girl crying and her parents crying and yelling, and wanting to take her away from us, thinking we were a bad influence on their daughter. But before long the parents said, "Why don't you take her? It looks like you've got better communication with her than we do anyway." One thing that parents notice is that our standards are very often the same as theirs. We have the same sentiments, for example, about wanting kids to straighten up. But we go about it in a slightly different way. Alienation doesn't happen. We have to tell them, some of these kids, "Look, you go to our machine shop and you steal our tools . . ." We get some of these kids off the street and they think they're going to do this kind of crap. And we tell them we are not the cops. "Who do you think we are, anyway? We're trying to do this thing here, and you should be helping out."

E: And if they don't, we send them back.

P: We had to send all three of the kids in our house back.

E: We can't keep anybody here who doesn't want to be here. It's got to be a cooperative thing.

P: We tell them that if they want to come back, that's okay, but for now go off and get some relativity. See what it's like in a detention home if that's what it takes. It's unfortunate; we don't want to have to do that, but in a lot of ways I think it's more beneficial to let the kids have that experience.

E: I wanted to mention one thing that we didn't quite finish when we were talking about how much time you spend with your kids and whether you can do other things in the community too. I personally work that out a lot, because I'm the secretary for The Farm correspondence; I cook at the school and do all kinds of stuff. So I'm gone four days a week. But the essence of the teaching here is it's the *quality* of the time you spend with your kids rather than how much time you spend that counts. If you're real with them and consistent in

your teaching while you're there—and it's meaningful—then they'll remember it.

RD: How do you deal with a problem that may develop with the kids at a community level?

E: The midwives are essentially in charge of child care and health care, and ladies' stuff on The Farm, you know, marriage counseling . . . because they bring the kids into the world and they are there to do the trip while the baby is being born. They take care of it from the time it is a baby, and they have a certain amount of vision from having delivered so many babies and dealing with life and death karma. Our midwives hold ladies' meetings. We all get together and decide on the standards, how we want it to be. We are always in communication.

P: Communication is one of the real cornerstones of the kind of social technology I was talking about earlier, in that you have to have complete, truthful, uninhibited communication among the folks before you can have any intelligence as a community, because the community mind works the same as an individual mind. If all the parts are in touch with each other and lines of communication are established, then there is coherent direction and unity of purpose in the community as a whole.

There are meetings, and then there is just the close friendship and agreement of all the people.

RD: I think agreement is really important. If somebody doesn't accept. . . .

P: Well, you have to allow for that, because if you don't, then you are going to squash any free thinking. And I think if you squash that, then you begin to get stagnant. A meeting has to stay open, but it's not a free-for-all. Order has to be maintained, and someone has to be in charge of the meeting. When somebody looks like he has made his point and he doesn't have to go any further, then that has to be brought out, too. You have to realize that the meeting can be a process of building agreement from grosser to more subtle levels, from the agreement to meet at all, to making effective decisions. The ladies' meetings are really valuable in helping the ladies see that some of their friends are having the same problems that they are; discussing things among themselves helps them deal with the problems.

RD: One of the things that I'm trying to understand here is . . . we get up in the morning and the first thing we do before the children wake up is meditate and do stuff like that—do yoga, all kinds of stuff to get ourselves straight. We do any rapping we have to do. Then the kids wake up and we take care of them, and so on. It seems to me that the kind of yoga that you're doing on The Farm is really a household yoga. It's a social yoga. And when you talk about having meetings, it's almost like reflecting back to each other what trips you see, and so on. And that's what I want to understand—what your path really is. It's interesting for me to hear that. I know one concept I read or I heard about years ago was the concept of the group head. I would like to hear more about that.

E: Well, I can give you examples, maybe. In our particular household, sometimes the standards get low and the ladies don't mop the floor every morning, and the germs are building up, and I'll see that and I'll say, "Okay, let's have a ladies' meeting. We can start to mop the floors every day. We've got to make sure that we don't change our diapers on the sofa . . ." And sometimes I sit down and make a list. Then we all have a meeting, and I say, "This is what I've noticed, and this doesn't feel cool to me," and usually everyone else has noticed it too, but you've gone so fast and you're truckin' so hard that you just don't take the time to . . . and usually everybody's in agreement, saying, "I noticed that, too; let's really try to get it together." So we do. Until it's time for another meeting to talk about it again.

RD: Are there cases where an individual or a couple of individual families within the larger household speak for themselves and form a separate group?

E: If they do, we say, "Hey man, are you antisocial?" Good-natured jibe, and then if that doesn't work we say, "Hey, are you serious about being part of the family? Or would you rather go do your own thing?" If they want to go do their own thing, that's fine.

RD: What are they expected to do then? Is there a place for them on The Farm or not?

E: Well, there is a certain standard that we have in our household that if you are going to live so close you have got to be in perfect agreement, so everybody can live harmoniously in this kind of situation. It takes a very tight agreement, you know. We have one couple in particular who tend to get a little out of it sometimes. It isn't that people can't go to their own room and do their own thing; you've got to do that to keep your head together, to keep your sense of family. But if people get to where they go up to their rooms and it feels real low energy and the agreement gets feeling kind of funky and you notice that the kids don't look too healthy or . . . it just starts falling apart, you can feel it—then you just tell them this is what it looks like. If you don't want to change—if they don't want to do that—we say "Okay, go find another place to live." Then they'll have to work that out with someone else, get stoned with someone else. Maybe it's just the chemistry of the house. Maybe they need to do another thing for a while. Maybe live by themselves and get their own agreement together.

RD: There's always space for them to do that if that's what they need to do? They don't get ostracized completely from the community?

E: No. Usually where we draw the line is violence. If somebody is getting into violence we say "No way!" We just can't have it; The Farm is a sanctuary.

VI

MIND MAKES AND MIND TAKES:
On Separation and Divorce

Divorce is always detrimental. It is just that in some cases a divorce may be less detrimental than staying together.

Murshid Moineddin Jablonski

In one sense married life may be looked upon as the intensification of most human problems. As such, it becomes the rallying ground for the forces of bondage as well as for the forces of freedom, the factors of ignorance as well as the factors of light. As the married life of ordinary persons is determined by mixed motives and considerations, it inevitably invites an uncompromising opposition between the higher and the lower self. Such opposition is necessary for the wearing out of the lower self and the dawning of the true Divine Self. Married life develops so many points of contact between two souls that severance of all connection would mean the unsettlement and derangement of practically the whole tenor of life. Since this difficulty of breaking away from one another invites and precipitates inner readjustment, marriage is really a disguised opportunity for the souls to establish a real and lasting understanding which can cope with the most complex and delicate situations.

Meher Baba, *Discourses*, 6th ed., 1:149–150

As Hazrat Inayat Khan points out, divorce may well be the best course of action:

Before one becomes sharp and the other blunt,
Before one is hot and the other cold,
Before one doubts and the other suspects,
Before one gives up his confidence and the other his trust,
It is time that they left one another.

Before one closes his eyes and the other his ears,
Before one turns his head and the other his back,
Before one talks and the other disputes,
Before one is in wrath and the other in rage,
It is time that they left one another.

Hazrat Inayat Khan, in *Vadan*

SOME THOUGHTS ON DIVORCE

A true marriage in which the partners selflessly offer themselves to one another can be the most beautiful vehicle to God—the soil in which universal love can grow and flourish. But married life can be a dull, monotonous contract bound up in all kinds of fear and resentment when it is based on exploitation rather than surrender and trust.

Making a yoga out of marriage, developing a spiritual attitude toward what could otherwise easily become a dulling and addicting ritual is not easy.

Most of us get married for a number of reasons, but most of them are superficial, devoid of any kind of inner commitment and real understanding of what marriage involves. Romanticism, insecurity, sexuality, family and social pressures, etc., are some of the usual motives for marriage. But it does not take long before the bubble bursts, before a dream full of hope becomes a nightmare. The romantic notions quickly dissolve; the longing that marriage will bring security is short-lived. The sexual mystique weakens and we are faced with several alternatives: we can separate and look for a new partner; we can stay together and suffer a life of imprisonment; or we can understand what marriage means in the deeper sense and *work* toward making it a path to God.

Unfortunately, most of us do not even know that the third alternative exists. Separation looks like the only escape, the only way out of the marital prison. But what we fail to realize is that the marriage is not the cause of our frustration—it is only a reflection of our own internal dissatisfaction, and running away from it is not going to solve anything. Human nature being what it is, in no time we find ourselves attached to new mates and going through the same or even worse ordeals.

This does not mean, however, that separation is never the appropriate action. There are extreme cases in which separation is the only appropriate action, and, in such cases, separation may take more courage than staying together. But the overwhelming majority of divorces result from immature motivations, with little understanding that we ourselves create our own prisons. Separating very often means that we want to hide—hide from the torment we create for ourselves with our own wrong attitudes.

When a man and woman marry they are beautiful to each other, but when they divorce they appear ugly to each other. Mind makes and mind takes.

Baba Hari Dass

One aspect of a real marriage is very well described by the Sanskrit word *tapas,* which means purification by fire. The demand in a marriage to relax one's self-centered desires is fierce, as just about every married couple will testify. That demand, when surrendered to, is tapas—purification by fire.

As a single person, one may have taken one's personal desires for granted, saying, "This is what I want for my trip." But in marriage, this attitude is bound to create tense moments as wills clash.

Unless total honesty, compassion, and the willingness to sacrifice self-centered desires take over here, resentment is inevitable. Resentment multiplied from day to day eventually will result in separation or divorce.

The demand in marriage is nothing less than for two separate wills to become united. This fusion of wills cannot come about by coercion, manipulation, or deceit on any level. It spontaneously comes through *mutual* compromise in a spirit of understanding. In short, a couple have to accept each other completely, and realize that through this acceptance they have created their own vehicle for self-transformation. As their wills unite, their spiritual path reveals itself. Acceptance is not easy, but it is nonetheless the foundation of spiritual work in the context of marriage.

Without wishing to make light of the many complex issues involved in separation and divorce, not to mention the misery in so many ongoing marriages, we are convinced that it is only when a couple mutually accepts the tapas aspect of their marriage that their marriage can offer them both spiritual development and satisfaction. This takes courage for each individual involved, desire for inner peace and contentment above all else, and a real willingness to sacrifice for the sake of the union.

BROKEN MARRIAGE: A PERSPECTIVE

P is a thirty-two-year-old accountant and tax consultant who, as a result of the break-up of his marriage, became intensely involved in yoga and meditation. After watching the process of his changes for about a year and a half during the compilation of this book, we finally interviewed him shortly before the manuscript was due to be handed in. Excerpts from that interview follow.

RD: P, you are a person whose marriage "failed." You've been separated for one and a half years now, and I'm wondering if you would share some relativity on what went wrong.

P: Our marriage failed because of a deep lack of acceptance of each other. It wasn't so much that we had different activities. It was more fundamental than that. It boiled down to the really fundamental thing of not accepting the marriage, of not accepting that there had to be surrender to each other. Finally, we came to a place where we knew we had to do this to make it work, but constantly we wouldn't accept it. We knew what we had to do; we knew where we were going wrong. I could give you a long list of all the areas where we differed, but it really came down, finally, to the question of acceptance. Neither of us really accepted the responsibility. And I see, in any relationship, that that's fundamental. That's the key. Once you're married, you've got no choice about it. You are married, that's a fact, and what do you have to do to make it work? You really just have to do it!

RD: Do you feel that the experience of your marriage helped you? What would your attitude be now in a relationship?

P: After we split up I was really in a pretty bad state. I was taking the kids on weekends then. This was a year and a half ago. Every second weekend I would come out to the farm and spend the weekend there, just visiting my sister and brother-in-law, Sharada and Sudarshan. I just had a social need for family, and I fulfilled it that way. It so happened that they were into a spiritual trip with Dharmasara, and satsang [a gathering, usually for devotions] was at the farm every second week, so that's how I got involved. And it just grew from there. That's turned out to be the greatest blessing in the world. So because of the pain that came from breaking up, I ended up doing sadhana.

As to what I learned in a more practical way that I would do in another relationship, there is a very subtle difference. In the previous relationship there was a lot of clarity. I knew all the time what was happening. So did my ex-wife. So I assume I would have the same clarity in a new relationship, the same discrimination as to whether something was good or not good. But I think that through doing sadhana I could develop the inner strength to be able to gracefully do what is right, which I couldn't do before, even though I saw what I should do. If you start a marriage on the right foot and work at positive things from the beginning, then bad patterns tend not to develop. The good ones develop. It can be incredible. I can see that. On the other hand, it could be like it was with me before where the negative patterns emerged. It just snowballed until I couldn't deal with it any more. Obviously it takes two people to make a marriage work, but I see now that one has to take responsibility for oneself. My inclination has now changed so that I wouldn't want to be involved with somebody who isn't into spiritual living and doing sadhana, which to me means I'd like to be with someone who is willing to take responsibility for working on themselves.

I'm willing to take responsibility for my own trips, but not for somebody else's. I'll try to help somebody else to work through their trips, and that's the kind of support that I see a marriage should give, to spiritual development, but it has to be a supportive thing with both sides working.

RD: You have two young kids. Can you share what you discussed with your ex-wife, and what you went through as the father figure phasing out of their lives to a considerable degree?

P: I never really had any problem there. We both recognized that whatever we would do, the kids would be our first concern. So it was really easy that way to work out an understanding. Our arrangement isn't that I have a *right* to see the kids, but rather that I have a *responsibility* to see them each week. Which is great for me. I love it. But it's more important for the kids. We always recognized that.

      The best thing that we could have done for the kids would have been to forgive and forget in a true sense and just go on living together, and try to develop a real marriage, but since we felt at that time that that wasn't possible—which really meant we didn't want to; we rationalized it that it wasn't possible—we felt that it would be better for the kids that they not be constantly exposed to our arguing and fighting. What it really comes down to is that for us it was all a cop-out.

RD: I think it's important to make a distinction. There are right reasons to stay in a relationship and there are wrong ones, too.

P: Oh, of course. I was just hanging on as a matter of attachment. Attachment to the marriage. There are all kinds of attachments involved. All kinds of ego trips: how different people will view me now that I'm separated, my parents and so on. The attachment of staying together for these external reasons was what was really holding us. We stayed together for a long time for no other reason.

      This thing, too, is really, marriage is no different from any other relationship. The same rules, the same ideas of controlling your desires, surrendering, and so on, apply in all relationships. To make any relationship successful you follow those rules. A marriage is, by its very nature, a closer relationship than most others. The only other difference is that you undertake a worldly responsibility that you don't necessarily have in other relationships, with some person you just know casually. You can walk away from him and the relationship is over—you have nothing to rub you. With a marriage you have a responsibility, and from the point of view of spiritual development, you have to fulfill it in an efficient and nonattached way. Otherwise you have constant thoughts and worries about it. It destroys whatever peace of mind you may have been able to develop.

RD: One thing I want to ask you. You use the phrase "control desires." Now, I want you to talk about what you mean about controlling desires in the sense that if you live out your desires you feed them.

P: Controlling desires is really a middle path of three things. One is fulfilling desires on the one side, the other side is suppressing desires.

RD: What do you mean by suppressing desires?

P: Not fulfilling them but still wanting them. Not giving in to them. Forcibly not fulfilling them. Confronting desires, controlling and eliminating desires, becoming desireless is really what I am talking about. You don't fulfill a desire because you know it is going to lead to more desires, and you don't want to have more desires. So you don't fulfill it. And at the same time, you don't hold onto it. You just give it up. That's really what I'm talking about. I don't think I can say it much more clearly.

VII
PRACTICES

A MARRIAGE WORKBOOK

AN ORIENTATION TO MARRIAGE AS SADHANA

As part of our research for *The Marriage and Family Book,* we compiled a "marriage questionnaire" which we sent to a number of New Age spiritual teachers and couples all over North America. The responses we received gave us a wealth of experience and knowledge to draw from, and provided us with many positive suggestions for the book.

One such suggestion was made by Reb Zalman Schachter and his wife Elana (see "Teachers and Teachings"). They suggested that the questions raised in the questionnaire were, in a sense, more important than the particular answers people gave. They said that, for themselves, the very exercise of focusing on the questions provoked a common reflection on the true meaning and purpose of their relationship. They acknowledged that they did not always share the same answers, but even the differences gave them a better idea of how the other thought or felt about a given subject.

That response, more than any answers we received, touched us, because above all else we wanted *The Marriage and Family Book* to be a book that we would share in more deeply with the reader than at the purely intellectual level.

Therefore, we invite you, the readers of *The Marriage and Family Book,* to follow Reb Zalman's suggestion: take the following questions and work on them—at the level of your own understanding and individual expectations of your relationship—and then get together with your partner to compare notes. See where you agree and where you don't. Use this process as a method to bring understanding into your relationship.

At the end of the question section you will find the responses of two well-known New Age spiritual teachers.

Questions

1. What is the spiritual purpose of marriage?

2. What do you see as being the current basis for most marriages?

3. Do you feel it is necessary for a couple to be legally married?

4. What is the importance of the marriage ceremony, and what is its inner meaning?

5. Why do you feel marriage is compatible with spiritual life?

6. What do you feel is the place of sex in a spiritual marriage?

7. Do you feel fidelity is necessary in marriage, and if so, why?

8. What do you feel are the necessary ingredients for a marriage in which both partners develop spiritually?

9. Do you feel that some kind of formal spiritual practice is of benefit to the harmony of marriage? If you do think so, what kind of practice would you recommend?

10. Do you have any recommendations for dealing with quarreling and misunderstanding in a spiritual marriage?

11. What should the attitude of the husband be toward the wife and the wife toward the husband?

12. What is the proper attitude toward money and possessions for householders?

13. What should a householder's attitude be toward working in the world?

14. When do you feel divorce is the best course of action?

15. When do you feel divorce is detrimental?

16. Do you feel ritual is of benefit to a harmonious family life?

____

____

____

____

____

____

17. What do you see as the reasons most people desire children?

____

____

____

____

____

____

18. What do you see as the reasons people do not desire to have children?

____

____

____

____

____

____

19. What is the spiritual purpose of having children?

20. When do you feel a couple should have children?

21. When do you feel a couple should not have children?

22. What is the best attitude for bringing up children?

23. What is the mother's duty in bringing up children?

24. What is the responsibility of the father in bringing up children?

25. How should parents work together in bringing up children?

____

____

____

____

____

____

26. What is the parents' responsibility for the formal education of their children?

____

____

____

____

____

____

27. What advice can you offer to single parents?

____

____

____

____

____

____

28. Do you feel that having only one parent affects children, and if so, how?

____

____

____

____

____

____

Responses

In the following responses to the questionnaire, the answers of Murshid Moineddin Jablonski will be identified as *J* and those of Roy Eugene Davis as *D*.

1. What is the spiritual purpose of marriage?

J. To effect links at levels deeper and higher than the normal links born of surfacial sexual outlooks. A spiritual marriage requires constant cultivation, just like a garden. While sexual play may serve many purposes, from gross to fine, the primary purpose is the continuance of the race. This takes real prayer and concentration on the part of husband and wife; every birth can be the birth of a Christ-child. The new age itself will come this way.

D. Marriage is an opportunity for two persons to share fully a relationship that can be based on love, mutual respect, and the recognition of innate divinity. It can afford the opportunity of working out subconscious patterns as well as bless those involved, and the world process as a result.

2. What do you see as being the current basis for most marriages?

J. Whatever it is, it is not deep enough in most cases. So many marriages tend to fall apart because one or both partners will not go through the trials of the psychic and emotional bodies that naturally arise during the course of any relationship that is being tested as to its worth. There is not enough mutual commitment to enduring the processes of purification which always come as a concomitant of character development—a normal and beautiful pattern of growth, if we will accept it.

D. I can't speak for most persons. But, most do desire union and a sharing of energies so that fulfillment and balance is experienced. This would be the underlying urge. Of course, psychological patterns often interfere and early traditional training distorts behavior.

3. Do you feel it is necessary for a couple to be legally married?

J. Not at all, but it can help in many instances. A legal bond tends to make things more definite.

D. It seems to me that marriage is a union of heart and soul, first of all. The legal steps are an adjustment to social rules and can contribute to stability for the family unit as well as harmony with society.

4. What is the importance of the marriage ceremony and what is its inner meaning?

J. The marriage ceremony is a ritual sealed with vows. The inner meaning is this: that we are identifying our present and future behavior with the vows we are enunciating. Mohammed has said: "Weakest among men is he who does not stick to his words." If we are going to make promises we must do so in a serious way, in a way which involves real commitment to our vows which, if they are real, have been made from the heart.

D. I see the marriage ceremony as a time of public agreement, personal commitment, and the opportunity to become attuned to higher energies. Souls working in relationship to God are sure to experience enrichment and the fulfillment of the dharma.

5. Why do you feel marriage is compatible with spiritual life?

J. Because the primary lesson is that we are one, we are a unity. We keep learning how imperfect life can be when we fall short of unity, but when the unity is experienced—especially unity in consciousness—then the divine spark is found, God is found. And when unity is experienced within the framework of family relations, it is possible to extend the discovery even further to include neighbors, fellow citizens, countrymen, even the whole of humanity.

D. Supreme Consciousness is playing all the roles. In this world (in all worlds) we have polarity. Fulfilled living is certainly in harmony with the spiritual life.

6. What do you feel is the place of sex in a spiritual marriage?

J. This is a question that may have a different answer at each stage in the maturity of a marriage. Sex may be very important as a form of expression in the early stages of a marriage, but as time goes on it may "wind down" as regards importance. Of course, sex is indispensable any time the subject of having a baby is current.

D. I feel that the male-female relationship is a sexual one. That is, a blending of energies and consciousness. If there is love and respect, then spontaneous sharing happens without guidelines or guidebooks. Egoless union is God loving God and God sharing with God.

7. Do you feel fidelity is necessary in marriage, and if so, why?

J. Yes, because a real marriage is a model for our relationship with the Beloved God. If we treat constancy as if it were of little real value, then we must be prepared to suffer a similar fate at the hands of the Beloved. In short, marriage is a preparation for the ultimate marriage of the soul with God.

D. Fidelity is necessary to maintain respect and trust. A deeper reason might be that outside relationships interfere with the quality of energy flow, much as the telepathic energy flow between guru and disciple is disturbed if there is not surrender, trust, and responsibility.

8. What do you feel are the necessary ingredients for a marriage in which both partners develop spiritually?

J. Love, hard work, an appreciation of modesty, joy in seeing your mate filled with light.

D. Compatible interests are essential ingredients for a marriage in which both partners develop spiritually. Also, trust, love, respect, maturity, philosophical understanding, and "space" for each to be individual in the relationship.

9. Do you feel that some kind of formal spiritual practice is of benefit to the harmony of marriage? If you think so, what kind of practice would you recommend?

J. If it doesn't become a trip, yes. The type of practice would depend upon the people involved. For some, more concentration on their children is all that would be required. For others, any number of practices could be helpful. The Divine Guidance should be sought in any case, and if a practice is indicated, then it may be given.

D. I feel the lifestyle should be compatible. Attention to the guidelines of yoga (yamas, niyamas [restraints, observances]) covers most of the subject.

10. Do you have any recommendations for dealing with quarreling and misunderstanding in a spiritual marriage?

J. "Apologize before the sun sets."

D. Quarreling has to be evidence of either weakness or a breakdown in communication. Open communication between mature persons will eradicate problems based on misunderstanding.

11. What should the attitude of the husband be toward the wife, and the wife toward the husband?

J. Husband to wife: protection, love, and respect.
Wife to husband: respect, love, and grace.

D. Each should see the other as a divine being, and honor, respect, and share in this light.

12. What is the proper attitude toward money and possessions for householders?

J. Could be different in each case. Some beings need to learn certain lessons, while other beings need to learn other lessons with regard to money and possessions. For some nonattachment may hold a key, and for others diligent concentration to increase their means may be more important.

D. Money and things are useful in the world. God is the substance of all form, anyway . . . so we are always dealing with an appearance of God's energy. Wise use of money and things, without hang-ups, is the way according to the seers.

13. What should a householder's attitude be toward working in the world?

J. Extremely tolerant. But he or she should also try and find the situation that is best, all things considered. For instance, a skinny vegetarian may look elsewhere than for a job as a bouncer in a bar. Or, conversely, a well-muscled contruction worker may take up a job other than taking shorthand in an air-conditioned office.

D. The world is the field for experience and opportunity. Therefore, one should be involved in a creative endeavor compatible with his ability and innate desire to contribute something useful. Working just to make money is not a sin; but one can fulfill destiny and still realize a flow of money.

14. When do you feel divorce is the best course of action?

J.

> Before one becomes sharp and the other blunt,
> Before one is hot and the other cold,
> Before one doubts and the other suspects,
> Before one gives up his confidence and the other his trust,
> It is time that they left one another.
>
> Before one closes his eyes and the other his ears,
> Before one turns his head and the other his back,
> Before one talks and the other disputes,
> Before one is in wrath and the other in rage,
> It is time that they left one another.

[Hazrat Inayat Khan, in *Vadan*]

D. When it is obvious that a man and woman are not truly mated and their fulfillment and growth is frustrated by the relationship.

15. When do you feel divorce is detrimental?

J. Divorce is always detrimental. It is just that in some cases a divorce may be less detrimental than staying together.

D. When one is injured or hurt by another. If there is open communication and love, the question will not arise.

16. Do you feel ritual is of benefit to a harmonious family life?

J. Vision is more important. However, rhythm and regularity in activities can provide a sound basis for harmony in any family setting.

D. Of course, ritual can be beneficial to a harmonious family life. Special times together, prayer and meditation together, grace before meals, many little gestures and rituals serve to focus on ideals and blend energy and intent.

17. What do you see as the reasons most people desire children?

J.   The reasons people see and the Divine Intention behind human reasoning are often very different matters. When the Divine Intention and a given couple's intuition coincide, then you have a tremendous possibility. You actually have a situation like Mary and Joseph, so to speak.

D.   Genuine desire to bring in a soul and provide learning and unfoldment opportunities . . . traditional beliefs . . . ego (unfortunately).

18. What do you see as the reasons people do not desire to have children?

J.   Mostly selfish, but that can be a safeguard, too. Sometimes people may not have children from other motives, e.g., Zero Population Growth, etc., but these motives may inhere more from psychological complexes than from actual or imagined environmental pressures.

D.   Not wanting to be responsible may be one reason. Another may be that one sees plenty of children available who need love and care without having to produce another. Perhaps one is not inclined by nature or karma to desire children.

19. What is the spiritual purpose of having children?

J.   To bring to earth souls of advanced evolution. Yet if the spiritual side is fulfilled, so also is the human aspect. It is impossible to separate purely human factors such as contentment while nursing, the joy of successful potty training, etc., from the spiritual values. We *have* children to experience life more fully; we *want* children in order to guarantee the future of humanity better than we were able.

D.   If the children can be provided for, the parents can look upon their children as bright spirits who can be assisted in their own unfoldment and destiny.

20. When do you feel a couple should have children?

J.   Only when God says so. This takes real listening.

D.   When they are mature enough to realize the responsibility.

21. When do you feel a couple should not have children?

J.   Whenever all systems are not "Go." It takes time for a couple to come around to the decision to have a child; it should never be forced.

D.   See above.

22. What is the best attitude for bringing up children?

J. As Jesus said, children can show us the way to Heaven. We, as adults, can gradually introduce the methods of concentration needed to make our way in the world. These two aspects should be balanced in the New Age.

D. Children are souls here for experience and support. We can bring out the innate potential with creative, loving attention to the process of education and sharing.

23. What is the mother's duty in bringing up children?

J. Hazrat Inayat Khan has said, "The mother is the first murshid." This means that the mother is the child's first spiritual teacher, which can be seen easily in the nursing process. The real duty of the mother is to keep her being pure of disturbing thoughts and emotions so that the child does not partake of life's shadows and thereby become impressed.

D. To be an example, a model. To educate in matters secular and spiritual with no traditional nonsense. To inform and teach by example the importance of working with others, nature, and God's will (the evolutionary pattern of nature).

24. What is the responsibility of the father in bringing up children?

J. To provide strength and positivity in the family setting. The question of active discipline may come in from time to time also. The father-image has been compared to the picture of the spiritual Master. The first few years the mother is all-important; then the father becomes more and more a part of the picture. (Responsibility is a good word to use in connection with the father's role.)

D. See above.

25. How should parents work together in bringing up children?

J. In the spirit of mutual support, bringing in as much as possible a balance of love, harmony, and beauty into the entire family scene.

D. See above. (And, above all, agree and work together for the common end.)

26. What is the parents' responsibility for the formal education of their children?

J. This varies quite a bit from culture to culture. Most New Age parents want a system of education that will insure their child of a normal and integrated pattern of growth. Some may wish their child to attend a school where God is given much consideration; others send their child to a more scientific school. Sufis try to combine these aspects as much as possible in the Seed Center schools.

D. I agree with the seers that one should have lower knowledge (knowledge of the relative worlds) and higher knowledge (knowledge of God and subtle matters which support and nourish the worlds).

27. What advice can you offer to single parents?

J. Keep looking for a proper mate. Short of this, it is often wise to engage a mother- or father-image on weekends just so that the child can relate to a member of the sex to which he or she belongs. No marriage-type relationship is indicated here; this is entirely for the child's benefit.

D. We are all life-giving spirits, rooted in God. With an understanding of mental principles (causation) and self-reliance, one who is single, with children, can handle life and the situations life presents with no great stress.

28. Do you feel that having only one parent affects children, and if so, how?

J. Definitely. It affects children to their very marrow not to have both parents present in their lives. More than any other class of people, children are outraged against the separation of their parents. They may not always say so; they may not know how to say so, but it is nonetheless written in the pages of their emotional makeup.

D. This depends upon the child and the influence of the parent on the child. It cannot all be environmental. Children also bring into this world their tendencies and urges.

COUPLES' PRACTICES

BASIC RELAXATION MASSAGE

Sometimes conflict arises in a relationship for some basic human reason: perhaps one or both of you are tired, uptight after a hard day, simply hungry, or genuinely sick, and before you quite realize what's going on you are snarling at each other!

Well, this isn't an attempt to smother conflict, which can be very constructive; rather it is a simple loving favor you may be in a position to give to your mate if he or she is temporarily down or at low energy.

Here's how you do it. The whole "massage" takes about five minutes. Make sure the room is warm.

Get your partner to lie on his (or her) stomach on the floor. Take off his shoes and socks.

Grab your partner's left foot with both hands and firmly but gently "shake" the tension out of the entire limb. Then do the same to the other leg.

Now grab hold of one foot with each hand, lift both legs a little, and then shake the legs together in harmony. If the legs are heavy, you may have to get a better grip by grabbing hold of them around the ankles.

Now ask your partner to turn over and lie on his back. With your left hand, "shake hands" with your partner and then gradually lift the entire left arm up perpendicular to the floor and shake out all the tension in the arm, shoulder, and back. Gently put the arm down again. Then do the same thing with the other arm.

Now cross your partner's arms across his (or her) chest and then grab each hand again but this time shake both arms together. Alternate your shaking motion to reach different areas.

Now tell your partner to take a deep breath, lift the upper back, neck, and shoulders off the floor, let his (or her) head loll back fully. Gently return his body to the floor.

Now quietly move behind your partner, rub your hands together briskly,

147

and then gently but firmly let your fingers "relax" the hollow part of the neck and the area where the skull meets the neckbone. After a few minutes, massage the scalp briskly, except around the temples which are very sensitive. Finally, place your right hand behind your partner's neck and your left hand over his (or her) heart area. Relax yourself completely, leaving your hands there without motion for about a minute. Allow your partner to continue lying on the floor for a few more minutes in complete silence.

PRELIMINARY HARMONIZATION: AN EXERCISE IN LISTENING

Many couples at times have problems in listening to each other. Sometimes one or both partners is guilty of projection or defensiveness, and therefore even the most basic communication is shut out—communion in the Spirit becomes impossible. But much "charge" between mates has to do either with misunderstanding, simply not listening, or downright poor communication.

We all know that communication is not confined only to words; therefore, this exercise should be as wholistic an attempt to communicate as possible. It should not be just an intellectual exercise in memory retention and repetition.

The exercise works like this:

Sit opposite each other. Close your eyes and do a preliminary harmonization together by chanting OM aloud repetitiously together for two or three minutes. Then just sit in silence for a few minutes.

Now mutually agree on who will first be the active and who the receptive partner for the purpose of this exercise. It's not really important who acts in which role as both of you will have a chance to play both roles. Now set a time limit (say, five minutes to begin).

Now look into each other's eyes. Active gives receptive a "message," starting each message by saying, "From my heart to your heart I want to share with you the following." The communication should be brief, to the point, and really express something you would like your partner to know. It can be a positive statement, an explanation, sharing a frustration or hurt, but it should be from "my heart to your heart."

The receptive listens attentively and makes no move to interrupt, to comment, defend, etc. When the active has indicated that he/she has finished, the receptive repeats his or her *understanding* of what the active said. The receptive makes no effort to defend, deny, or affirm what the active has said; he or she merely repeats back an understanding of the active's words. The active then either acknowledges that the receptive has understood satisfactorily or once again explains. Receptive is attentive and once again repeats back the understanding. When the active is satisfied that he/she has communicated what was intended, the roles are reversed.

This exercise can be a lot of fun, but can also prove extremely useful during crisis times (if you choose to use it with real honesty and openness).

CONTEMPLATION ON THE PATH OF MARRIAGE

One of the most difficult, yet most essential aspects of marriage is surrender, a willingness to let go into the point of view of self that includes "both of us." This movement should not become an egocentricity that develops into a "we two" versus the world, but rather a harmony that provides the ground for going beyond individual selfishness through a mutual attitude of relaxed compromise.

The following practice includes mudras (positions of the body that channel energy and cultivate spiritual states of mind) as well as contemplations which correspond with each mudra. When these are practiced by both partners together, the exercise becomes an expression of mutual surrender and an agreement to cultivate virtue in the relationship.

Clasp your hands together in front of your heart, inhale deeply, and, chanting an OM, bow to the self in each other. This greeting is called "namaste," which means "I honor the light within you."

1. The Mudra of Action

Method: Sit cross-legged facing each other. Stretch your right hand, palm facing inward, and touch the floor with your fingertips. Join the index finger and the thumb of your left hand together, and rest your hand on your left knee.

Contemplation: We are both channels for God's will, and can only act clearly when we perform His will, and do not act exclusively from our own motivations. We can row our boat together across the sea of life.

2. The Mudra of Serenity

Method: Raise the right hand, palm facing outward. Stretch the arm downward, fingers pointing toward the floor.

Contemplation: Everything is always perfect exactly the way it is. There is no need for uptightness. Though we recognize the personality flaws in each other, we accept each other, and we accept our situation as it is. We renounce our habits of dissatisfaction, melancholia, and anger. We trust and accept responsibility for ourselves as individuals.

3. The Mudra of Humility

Method: Cup the palms of each hand over each breast, bend the head slightly, and bow forward very gently toward each other.

Contemplation: Only in the deepest humility can we two become one. When we are in humility, it is because we have forgotten ourselves, our petty concerns and insecurities. In humility, we are able to trust each other and everyone else. In humility, we meet in total equality, neither higher nor lower, superior nor inferior.

4. The Mudra of Truthfulness

Method: Rest the backs of both hands on the knees. Join the index finger and the thumb together to form a circle on each hand.

Contemplation: In every gesture, movement, and action we make we will strive to live truth. There is only One, and therefore when we lie, either subtly or overtly, we lie to our very self. We will strive to make every action and response in this relationship come from the foundation of this truth.

5. The Mudra of Equanimity

Method: Bend both arms at the elbow with the palms open and facing upward, as though your hands were a scale.

Contemplation: Equanimity is balance. We will strive toward balance in every aspect of our being; we renounce emotional excesses and indulgences; we are whole and balanced, at peace with ourselves and with the process of life.

6. The Mudra of Detachment

Method: Stretch the arms out, fingertips touching the ground, palms facing outward.

Contemplation: We will not hide from each other, or anyone, and we will not avoid any situation—but we will strive to remain aloof from self-importance. We will strive to perform everything that we are called upon to do as channels for His will.

7. The Mudra of Courage

Method: Make both hands into fists and cross your arms in front of your chest.

Contemplation: We have the strength at any time to take full responsibility for ourselves. We do not have to depend on anyone else for our happiness and security. We accept joyously the opportunity to grow and to leave the past behind.

8. The Mudra of Sobriety

Method: Place both hands on the knees, palms facing downward.

Contemplation: We will strive always for objectivity and proportion in our views of the world. We will strive to not indulge our own subjective view of life and thereby cut ourselves off from others, and from the flow of life around us.

9. The Mudra of Innocence

Method: Cup your hands together in the prayer mudra. Bow slightly toward each other.

Contemplation: We will strive to clear ourselves from moment to moment, to be cleansed of expectations, judgment, and desire. We will strive to see as a babe sees and to take joy in our lives.

HARMONIZING THROUGH BREATH AND MOVEMENT

Focusing the mind on breath and movement is one of the most powerful ways to come into harmony.

Sit facing each other. Chant OM and bow to each other. Close your eyes and sit quietly for a few minutes.

After a few minutes, open your eyes; then, with your right palm facing down and your left palm facing up, place your hands on top of each other.

Close your eyes again. Now, slowly and gently, begin to move your arms in unison with your breathing pattern.

As you inhale, gently pull your left arm toward your body, while pushing your right arm away from you toward your partner. Then, when you exhale, reverse the arm movement, left arm moving toward your partner and right arm being drawn back to yourself.

Now allow your breathing to become more subtle. Guide each other using pressure in your hand movements. Communicate more subtly, sensitively paying attention to the subtle messages your partner may be giving through his/her movements.

Merge through your breathing, hand movement, and concentration. When you feel you have established a deep rapport, stop the hand movements. Simply sit together and enjoy your harmony.

MEDITATION OF COMMUNION

Sit facing each other. This exercise is best done after the preceding "Harmonization through Breath and Movement." When you both feel that your breath is harmonized and natural, open your eyes and gaze into the area of the third eye in the center of each other's forehead.

After a few minutes of concentration, place your left hands over your heart region and your right hand gently on your partner's neck near the jugular vein.

The contact is very gentle. Maintain this physical posture and enter meditation together.

MEDITATION TO HARMONIZE THE AURA

Sit back to back, spinal cords touching all the way up. Find a position where you are not weighing on each other, conjoining magnetic fields, auras, souls. Breathe in at the same time. Whoever wants to breathe in first backs his head lightly against his partner; then separate the heads slightly. Hold the breath, hold heads against one another; then whoever wants to start exhaling first just separates from his partner.

When the heat and power of the spines get too much, edge away a little bit from one another. You'll find the right distance. Then you'll start experiencing a current of magnetism rising from the bottom of the spine to the top of the head. Then you've got it.

Be conscious of being one aura. When you separate heads, that one aura is radiating in two directions. The stronger the power, the more distance you will have to hold from each other.

The woman's crown is like a chalice; the man's aura is like a fountain. You will find this feeling of this junction within one aura like an eagle with two heads. It must be very harmonious, the two rhythms making one. When this happens, lift your consciousness together above the body. You may get the experience of high flight.

Pir Vilayat Inayat Khan, Toward the One, pp. 672–73

EXPANDING INTO NEW AREAS OF HARMONY

In the preceding exercises the concentration has been on consciously bringing two separate energy fields into a synchronous whole. Yet these exercises at best can reflect only a relatively small part of a couple's lives together. The real challenge is in integrating this consciously created harmony into the many other areas of your intertwined lives. In the deepest sense this will mean applying yoga, or union, to your everyday actions.

It is almost as if we are instruments of the Divine and as we open ourselves at each level He plays through us yet another chord of His lila, His divine dance.

Here are some other areas into which your consciously created harmony should be expanded:

Lifestyle harmony
Sexual harmony
Emotional harmony
Intellectual harmony
Creative harmony
Commitment harmony
Communication harmony
Spiritual harmony
Aesthetic harmony
Recreational harmony
Working harmony

Learn to treat each other like the Gods and Goddesses you are.

VIII
THE WEDDING CEREMONY : A Mystical Perspective

INTRODUCTION TO THE WEDDING CEREMONY
SPOKEN BEFORE A WEDDING BY PIR VILAYAT INAYAT KHAN

I always feel that a wedding is a very sacred rite and, for myself, I feel a very great responsibility in being party to uniting people. Although marriage is a commitment which a couple make themselves, sometimes my intuition tells me that they will not be happy together. It seems a terrible thing to say to people; even though one realizes the implications, one does hesitate to say something of that nature. I know it is a problem that quite a number of gurus face.

Many gurus say, "Well, why not wait a little bit?"—implying that if there are basic differences, they will come up, they will manifest in the course of time. Sometimes, though, I feel that it is not right for a person in my position to send away an experience, even if it may be an unpleasant one. That may be the way a couple learns, so I do not always express my feelings about situations. I think that sometimes a difficult relationship is a wonderful test, and one that helps people to work with themselves and with each other to improve themselves and their relationship. For that reason, I don't always believe in relieving people of their load.

On the other hand, when I feel the people are wonderfully suited, then it is a very great joy to perform the wedding ceremony.

Marriage is a contract between two people, but that contract is with God, as a pledge. The pledge is "I will." The way in which a couple says "I will" to each other differs, of course, in different cultures. I, for example, am not using exactly the same pledge that was used in the past. I am rather using the phrase "Will you stand *by* one another under all circumstances?" And the reason is that I think this is really the essence of a relationship.

In broader terms, to stand by one another is the essence of the relationship of friendship. To stand by one another is a kind of loyalty of the spirit. It means, for example, that one doesn't speak subversively against the person with whom one is married to someone else if one is displeased with that person. That's what I call standing by one another.

Another aspect of accepting the marriage pledge is that if for some reason the ways part, the husband, for example, feels morally and financially responsible to his wife. And it could even be the other way around. If there are children, then of course there is a great responsibility. The reason for my caution about this is because when all is well a marriage can be a most wonderful relationship, and should last one's whole life; but a lot of people jump into it without knowing the implications. One doesn't always know what the factors are that draw people to the point of deciding to marry. It might be even just a physical attraction, and that isn't enough to keep people together. It might be an affinity at the psychological level, it could even be an affinity at the spiritual level, and still not be effective at a purely human level. People do make mistakes in life, and if the relationship does not turn out to be satisfactory for both, it can be a terrible prison. And that is why in the New Age people are not against responsible divorce, because if two people are unhappy together because of fundamental differences in outlook, and they would be more suited to other partners, it is a very great shame if they cannot change over to other partners. A relationship without a strong common goal on every level can make a person very bitter if he or she feels imprisoned in that relationship.

A relationship should always be inspiring, it should always be creative, and it should also renew us in our love, so that we never take each other for granted. Every day, every moment, we discover a new dimension of the relationship. And then, of course, it is wonderful.

THE WEDDING CEREMONY OF THE SUFI ORDER IN THE WEST

On the altar, arranged in the ordinary way, are placed a cup of corn and the wedding rings. Bride and bridegroom sit in the first row, the bridegroom at the right side of the bride. At the right of the bridegroom sit the two best men and at the left of the bride the two bridesmaids.

The service is held until after the sermon and the cherag (standing in the center and facing the congregation) invites bridegroom and bride to rise.

Cherag to bridegroom: *Do you ask for the hand of this maiden (or lady) offering her in exchange your most sincere love?*
Bridegroom: *I do.*
Cherag: *Will you keep true to her, serve her, sympathize with her under all conditions throughout your life?*
Bridegroom: *I will.*
Cherag: *Will you consider this maiden (lady) who is to be your wife as the most sacred trust given to you by God?*
Bridegroom: *I will.*
Cherag to best man: *Will you be witness to what — has promised?*
Each best man: *I will.*
Cherag to bride: *Do you accept — as your husband, sincerely, in devotion?*
Bride: *I will.*

Cherag to bridesmaids: *Will you be witness to what — has promised?*
Each bridesmaid: *I will.*

The bride and bridegroom remain standing before the cherag, but turn
their faces to each other. The cherag, holding the hands of both, repeats:

*Toward the One, the Perfection of Love, Harmony, and Beauty, the Only Being,
united with All the illuminated Souls who form the Embodiment of the Master, the
Spirit of Guidance, I unite you both in marriage, one to another, that this link [the
cherag puts on the rings] may be an everlasting bond, asking for your good health,
long life, and prosperity, Happiness, and the Blessings of God be with you for ever
and evermore. Amen.*

The cherag says to the congregation: *Let us pray for them.*
The congregation rises while bride and bridegroom kneel down facing the
altar. The cherag stands in the midst before the altar facing bride and groom.
The prayer is repeated:

*O Thou, the Creator, Lord, Master, and Sustainer of our lives, pour Thy Love and
Thy Light on this couple who marry under Thy divine protection. May the harmony of
Thy divine nature unite them, may compassion kindle their hearts, send on them Thy
divine blessing that they may be surrounded with good health, prosperity, success,
and happiness, and may they glorify Thy Name now and for evermore. Amen.*

Bride and bridegroom rise.
The cherag gives them each a handful of corn saying: *Pour the seed of the
Divine Message upon the world.*
He lays his hands on the head of each saying: *God bless you.*
Then they rise and the cherag says the *Khatum* and gives the blessing to
the congregation.

THE JEWISH WEDDING CEREMONY
ACCORDING TO THE TEACHINGS OF REB SCHLOMO CARLEBACH AND REB ZALMAN SCHACHTER (COMPILED BY SUDARSHAN FILKOW)

Preparation

In Jewish tradition, preparation for the marriage ceremony is as important as
the ceremony itself. The occasion is seen as the actualization of an event
which was ordained in heaven. The participants, by careful preparation,
invoke God's presence and uplift themselves to meet Him.

The Fast

The day of the wedding, the bride and groom fast until they drink the first cup of wine during the ceremony. It is a way in which the bride and groom set this day apart from other days to build toward that special moment of sharing the first sacramental cup of wine together.

Reading of the Torah

According to Chassidic tradition it is said that God wrote the Torah before he created the world and when it came time to create the world he looked into the Torah to follow what he was supposed to do. The groom is about to embark upon a totally new life and together with his bride they will create a new world. So the Saturday before the wedding the groom is called to the Torah so he may "look inside" for guidelines for his future creation.

The Ritual Bath (Mikveh)

"Mikveh" itself means a gathering of water. Traditionally a mikveh is a pool where there is a natural gathering of water such as rainwater or melted ice gathered in surroundings which are as natural as possible. Its special purpose is for people to come and dip themselves in it in order to purify themselves. It is very much like a ghat in India. Most synagogues have a mikveh, but one can be created wherever there is natural flowing water and natural surroundings.

The rite of mikveh requires that the person about to take a mikveh take a bath beforehand, comb hair, cut fingernails, etc., so that every foreign substance is removed, so there is even preparation for this event.

In the mikveh the bride or groom dips once in each direction. Each direction represents one letter of the divine name "YHVH," recognizing that God's presence is everywhere.

Going into the water symbolizes surrender, ego death, release from all worldly attachments (impurities). On the highest level it symbolizes immersion in the divine element, a recognition that we are not separated from God. On a spiritual level we are always in the mikveh.

Clothing

The bride and groom should wear any special clothing they may have as well as any special prayer garments in order to further sanctify the occasion. Traditionally, the groom wore the white shawl which he wore on the high holy days and in which he would be buried so that at the wedding he has the sense of wearing his "eternal garment."

The Talus

The talus is the prayer shawl which the men wrap themselves in when praying. It is a place where a person can withdraw into the presence of God. Traditionally, the bride gives a talus to the groom as a wedding gift and it is used as the canopy under which the bride and groom stand during the ceremony.

The talus is very big, it's like a garment you wrap yourself in but it's not made to measure. It means, on one hand, it is infinite—God is not made to measure. On the other hand it is small, but still not made to measure. It is the most infinite, finite thing there is. It is like prayer itself. You think you are praying for something finite, something specific, but it's not true. When you really pray you connect yourself with the infinite. The value is a special symbolic gift. In our lives we meet many people we love, but only one person who gives us a talus of peace.

Reb Schlomo Carlebach

The Chupa

The chupa (canopy) means "that which covers; that which floats above." It symbolizes the home the bride and groom will make and live in as a house of God. It represents a covering over a sacred place. At one time the chupa was the canopy over the bed in which the bride and groom would consummate the marriage and the place where they would make love during their marriage.

Entering under the chupa is the moment when the roving eye stops roving for other partners, for it is the moment of coming together.

The chupa represents the divine throne. Many illustrations of the divine throne in kabbalistic literature show it as being surrounded by four characters from the Zodiac—the lion, the bull, the eagle, and the aquarian. Four appropriate persons—a taurus, a scorpio, a leo, and an aquarian—should be chosen to hold the four staves which support the canopy during the ceremony so that the energy of all the corners of the world is represented.

It is said that the divine name floats over the chupa, and it is here that all the preparation will give rise to the Divine being brought down.

The Witnesses

The witness or witnesses to the signing of the marriage contract should be chosen carefully. He or she should be someone close to the bride and groom, someone whom they can respect and trust so they can go to the witness during difficult times and say "You were the witness to our vows. Now we need your help to work this through."

The Marriage Contract

The main document contains the essentials relating to the marriage. In it the groom and bride state their wish to marry each other. The groom pledges to provide for his bride, feed her, take care of her, and do all the things that a husband has to do no matter what the sacrifice or cost.

According to Chassidic teaching the parchment on which the contract is written is white fire and the letters black fire, so, in signing, the bride and groom are writing black fire upon white fire and are saying "I will feed your body and sustain your soul with truth."

The Auxilliary Document

Because Jewish law set out certain conditions for divorce it was common for this document to set out additional conditions which the bride and groom agreed would govern with respect to separation, annulment, and divorce, and generally at what point one of the partners could legitimately say that the marriage was at an end. Today this document can be a personal marriage document which sets out all their vows and intentions regarding their marriage and their pledge to honor and respect those vows.

The Guests

The task of the guests is to assist in uplifting the atmosphere of the wedding, by wearing special clothing, by chanting, by concentrating their effort, attention, and consciousness before and during the ceremony, and by directing their prayers to the couple to have a happy marriage, blessed with happy children, to find their livelihood, and to increase their understanding of each other.

The Veil

After the signing of the contract and before the beginning of the ceremony, the bride is veiled.

The Bible says that when Isaac met Rebecca, Rebecca covered her eyes. Why did she cover her eyes? To tell him that their relationship was beyond the level of seeing. When a couple gets married, the bride covers her eyes. Her seeing is on the level of longing. The groom lifts the veil after he puts the ring on her finger and looks into her eyes to see what no one else can see.

If a couple only know each other by what they see, then there is no real connection between them. If they see in each other all the things that nobody else sees, this means they really love each other and they see the Almighty put them together before they were born.

Reb Schlomo Carlebach

According to Chassidic teaching, the moment of the veiling is also the moment in which holy eyes are given to the bride, special mother's eyes with which to watch over her children. It is the moment at which she is connected to the place from which her children will come, and at the time the bride walks down the aisle to the canopy, one great rabbi said, all her children and grandchildren till the end of their generations are walking behind her.

The Ceremony

After the bride and groom are under the canopy the ceremony begins. There is an invocation:

> He who is supremely mighty,
> He who is supremely blessed,
> He who is supremely sublime,
> May he bless the groom and the bride.

Blessed art thou, Lord our God, King of the universe, who createst the fruit of the vine.

Blessed are thou, Lord our God, King of the universe, who has sanctified us with thy commandments, and commanded us concerning illicit relations; thou hast forbidden us those who are merely betrothed, and permitted us those who are married to us through consecrated wedlock. Blessed are thou, O Lord, who sanctifiest thy people Israel by consecrated wedlock.

The three aspects of the Divine are called down. The rabbi says: "He who is supremely mighty" [etc., see marriage service].

Then comes the first blessing, over the wine: "Blessed art thou, Lord our God, King of the universe, who created the fruit of the vine." The invocation continues: "Blessed art thou," etc.

The bride walks around the groom seven times in a clockwise direction. This direction represents a rising, a going upward, as it is said that it is the nature of the bride that she is moving upward to receive the divine energy. It is the nature of the groom to focus energy. If he wishes to walk around the bride seven times, he moves in a counter-clockwise direction, bringing down energy from above. The bestower and the receiver bring the divine energy together and meet in the middle.

Another interpretation of this is that the walking around the partner symbolizes the building of a holy wall around the partner to protect him or her in the days to come. One time for every day of the week—to remind us that marriage is not part time but twenty-four hours a day, every day of the week.

The Ring

The groom places the ring on the forefinger of the bride's right hand and says: "With this ring you are consecrated to me in accordance with the law of Moses and Israel." (This formula can be varied so that the woman responds, or the woman begins and the groom responds. Additional words, in keeping with the marriage contract, may be spoken.) At this time the males present could join hands and concentrate all their energies into the groom, and the women into the bride.

In Hebrew there are two words for ring. *Tebad* has the same root letters as *nature*. So what is being said is "Behold, thou art consecrated unto me with this nature, with this imprint." The ring symbolizes a great seal being set upon the heart of the bride, sealing forever the transformation from the unmarried state to the state of "wed-lock," matrimony.

The second word for ring is *gal-gal*, which means "I, infinite wheel, reincarnation." The giver of the ring is saying "We are married for all eternity. I might have to come back and I love you so much I want you to come with me." And the receiver is saying "I love you so much that if you have to come back I will come with you." The ring is first placed on the forefinger and is later placed on the regular ring finger. Each finger has a name and special significance in Kabbalah. The forefinger is the pointing finger and is held up as a sign to show everyone that the bride is married.

The marriage contract is now read. The groom gives it to the bride or contracts are exchanged. The giver of a contract is saying "I have written myself into this contract. It is as close as I can possibly come right now to showing you my commitment to you." One teaching says the giver is saying "Behold I have given myself to you in this document."

Seven blessings are then recited, again one for every day in the week so each day of the marriage should be filled with blessing.

The first:

Blessed art thou, Lord our God, King of the universe, who createst the fruit of the vine.

This refers to and calls down on the couple the aspect of God's grace and bounty.

Here the groom lifts the veil, looks at the bride, and they both drink from the cup of wine. The unveiling is a very important part of the ceremony. Again it is part of seeing, of recognizing, not only the beautiful aspects, the divine aspects of the partner, but also all the not-so-beautiful, not-so-divine aspects that are present, but which are accepted as well.

The second:

Blessed art Thou, Lord our God, King of the universe, for creating everything and filling it with so much glory and honor.

Everything is created for His glory: "Thank you for the glory of being alive to experience all the things which you are giving us."

This is the blessing of rigor. The bride and groom concentrate their strength into it to bring about a weld between them and to offer their lives for the glory of God, to sanctify their home, make it a temple, and serve God in it.

The third:

Blessed art Thou, God, King of the universe, who created mankind.

This blessing is related to beauty.

This is a good point to have the parents of the bride and groom involved, for chances are that when their son or daughter was born this blessing was not said so it is a good time for them to get back to and reflect on their creation.

The fourth:

Blessed art Thou, God, King of the universe, who created man in Your own image and who created woman to eternally be beside him.

What we are really saying is "Thank you, God, not only for creating man but for endowing him with eternal, ever-building, creative force so that man can create another being in your image."

This blessing is related to energy. It acknowledges the tremendous eternal, building creation. The bride and groom are like the waist of an hourglass. The ancestors of the bride and groom have come through to them and will come through them to their descendants.

They are a narrow passage between past and future. Energy must pass between them so all their ancestors can become their descendants, that is, the building forth and forever building forth. In a real way it is saying "Thank you, God, for that which renews itself eternally and for the power that is nature."

The fifth:

May Zion exult at the joyful reunion of her children in Jerusalem, Blessed art thou, O Lord, who causest Zion to rejoice in her children.

This blessing is related to the attribute of splendor, glory. It is saying "Don't forget, there is a context to everything you do—everything is related to God." It is the attribute of Aaron, the attribute of priesthood, the Temple. It is saying "Remember—whatever we do is in the context of God's glory."

The sixth:

Give joy to these two loved companions the same way you gave joy to Adam and Eve in the Garden of Eden. Blessed art thou, O Lord, who gives joy to the bridegroom and bride.

This blessing has the attribute of begetting. Before the fall Adam and Eve did not even know there was such a thing as hate. Their experience of love was not like the love we experience. So we bless the bride and groom so their love will be on the level it was in Paradise. It also is a reminder that after all the rejoicing is over and the guests are gone and they are alone together, only God can ensure that they will continue to rejoice and celebrate together.

The seventh, and final blessing is:

Blessed art Thou, Lord, our God, King of the universe, who created bridegroom and bride, joy and gladness, delight and cheer, love, harmony, and all the different kinds of happiness, peace, and companionship. May these joyous sounds and the sound of joyous wedding celebrations sound and spread throughout the world. Thank you, O Lord, who gives joy to bride and bridegroom.

The final blessing is followed by the groom's breaking the wine glass with his foot. This is to recall the difficulties of the past and to remember the fragility and temporalness of everything—that there will also be hard times ahead. It also symbolizes that they will not need this glass again for the breaking is a seal of the marriage.

This ends the ceremony. The chupa may be lowered over the bride and groom for a moment or two so that they can be alone before turning to meet the guests.

Traditionally, at this point the bride and groom are taken to a room where they can be in private for a few minutes. This gives the opportunity for the symbolic "consummation" of the marriage.

Reb Nachman says that people come to a wedding and then they walk out. One says, "It was a beautiful wedding; I liked the food." Another says, "I liked the music." Another says, "I met a lot of good friends there." Those people weren't really at the wedding. Then someone walks out and says, "Baruch Hashem [Blessed be the Name], thank God those two got together!" He was there at the wedding.

HEBREW WEDDING BLESSING
TRANSLATED BY RABBI DANIEL SIEGEL

We acknowledge the Unity of all, expressing our appreciation for this wine, symbol and aid of our rejoicing.

We acknowledge the Unity of all, recognizing our responsibility to play the parts assigned to us, to make our lives meaningful and our relationships open and beautiful. We are grateful for this opportunity to publicly express our feelings and intentions.

We acknowledge the Unity of all, expressing our appreciation for this wine, symbol and aid of our rejoicing.

We acknowledge the Unity of all, realizing that each separate moment and every distinct object points to and shares in this oneness.

We acknowledge the Unity of all, recognizing and appreciating the blessing of being human.

We acknowledge the Unity of all, realizing the special gift of awareness that permits us to perceive this unity and the wonder we experience as a man and a woman joined together to live as one.

May rejoicing resound throughout the world as the homeless are given homes, persecution and oppression cease, and all people learn to live in peace with each other and in harmony with their environment.

From the source of all energy we .call forth an abundance of love that envelops this couple. May they be for each other lovers and friends and may their love partake of the same innocence, purity, and sense of discovery that we imagine the first couple to have experienced.

We acknowledge the Unity of all, and we highlight today joy and gladness, bridegroom and bride, delight and cheer, love and harmony, peace and companionship. May we all witness the day when the dominant sounds throughout the world will be these sounds of happiness, the voices of lovers, the sounds of feasting and singing.

Praised is love; blessed be this marriage. May the bride and bridegroom rejoice together.

MARRIAGE IN HINDU RELIGION
BY BABA HARI DASS

When the first being on the earth desired to be several, immediately a female form similar to him appeared. By their union, creation expanded. Probably that was the first marriage on the earth.

Among Hindus the basis of marriage is the spiritual unification of the couple by sacred mantras. The bride and groom are considered to be male and female forms of God. They are decorated as god and goddess, and several rituals are performed to join them in marriage.

The rituals are mainly symbolical. In ancient times symbolism played a very important part in human life; all over the world there were similarities of ideas in symbolism. The rites and rituals are performed to convince the couple that male and female are married.

Before and after a marriage, couples are supposed to avoid touching or seeing certain things which are considered to be dangerous, and conversely to seek out other things which are supposed to bring good luck. All kinds of good and bad omens are seen at the time of marriage. For example: seeing a black cat is a bad omen; seeing a woman carrying a bucket of water is good. The bride is placed on a bull's hide, which is a symbol of fertility; she sits, or steps, on a stone as a symbol of firmness. All such kinds of rituals are celebrated in the performance of marriage.

The earliest references to marriage are found in the *Rig Veda* and *Atharva Veda*. The period of Vedic time may go back to the time between 1500 and 1000 B.C. Domestic rituals are also found in the *Dharma Sutras,* which explain marriage ceremonies in detail. The *Dharma Sutras* are the oldest law books of the Indians; they include books of instructions on spiritual and secular law. The period of the *Dharma Sutras* is 600–300 B.C. In addition, the *Artha Shastra* of Kantilya, the most important early Indian manual of statecraft and secular law, *Manu Smriti* (Code of Manu), and a few other smrities (scriptures) offer good references to marriage in Hindu culture.

In the *Dharma Sutra* period, eight types of marriage are mentioned, which are:

1. *Brahma.* In the Brahma method the father of the bride looks for the groom. The marriage is settled by having their horoscopes cast. The groom should be of the same caste; his family, character, education, and health are investigated. Then the father gives his daughter, decorated with ornaments, as a gift to the groom. This is one of the orthodox and approved forms of marriage. It is possible, also, for the bridegroom to ask for the hand of the bride.

The father has the obligation to give a dowry for his daughter to the husband.

The bride has no part in the choice of her husband. It is entirely in the hands of her father. If the father is dead, then an uncle or an older brother selects a groom in the same manner.

2. *Daiva.* In this method the selection of the groom is made by the father or guardian and the marriage is settled as in the Brahma method. However, the bride is given as a part of the sacrificial fee to the officiating priest, who performs a sacrifice for her father. And then the regular marriage ceremony is performed.

In Daiva method of marriage the bride has no choice of her husband—it is made by her father or a guardian.

3. *Prajapatya.* In the Prajapatya form of marriage the groom is selected by the father as in Brahma and the bride is given as a gift to the bridegroom, or he is requested to accept the bride. But there is a condition implied, which is

that they both should never cease to perform dharma together. To perform dharma together means that the bridegroom cannot enter any other asrama. [There are four kinds of asrama: brahmacharya (student), grihastha (household), vanprastha (hermit), sannyasa (renunciate).] Also, he should not take another wife. Whereas in a Brahma marriage, both perform a spiritual life, but they can change their asrama.

4. *Arsa.* In the Arsa form of marriage the bridegroom looks for a bride. When he finds one, he presents the bride's father, or her guardian, with a bull and a cow. Presenting a cow and bull is a mark of honoring the father and family of the bride. It also symbolically says, "We want to be a couple like this cow and bull."

The father or guardian has the authority to accept or reject the marriage proposal. The bride does not have any choice in the selection of the bridegroom.

The difference between Arsa and other types of marriages is that the choice is made first by the suitor and then the parents' consent is needed.

All these four are orthodox forms of marriage and approved by lawgivers. The rites and rituals of the marriage ceremony are the same for all.

The other four forms are independent and the bride can be acquired in various ways:

5. *Raksasa.* Raksasa is a form of marriage in which the bride is forcibly taken away. This practice was started by Kshatriyas, men of the warrior race, who did not want to accept a gift but wanted to win a bride by their bravery. Several battles were fought by brave Kshatriyas only to get a bride. Although this method is not approved of in the *Dharma Sutras,* the bride was given a legal status after she was won by the bridegroom.

Still, in certain parts of India among the Kshatriyas, this method is in vogue in a symbolic form. The people from the bridegroom's side dress as warriors and dance with swords and shields. They beat wardrums and blow conches all the way to the bride's house, carrying a huge red flag in front, which is a symbol of challenge. When they bring the bride back, they carry a white flag, which is a symbol of peace.

6. *Asura.* The Asura marriage involves the bride's being purchased by the suitor, who pays a suitable price to the parents or guardians of the bride. This method was common among Vaisyas (business class) and Sudras (serving class). There were no exact rules about the price for the bride—it was settled by the parents of both sides.

The Asura marriage is also disapproved of by the *Dharma Sutras* and considered one of the inferior forms of marriage. Although selling of daughters is disliked by the people, yet society accepted it and the bride was considered eligible to take part in any rites and rituals in the society.

7. *Gandharva.* In the Gandharva marriage the male and female fall in love

and get married. They don't seek consent of their parents. Gandharva marriage is based on sexual desires for each other. Male and female get involved sexually and then they decide to marry. This kind of marriage can happen within the caste or intercaste. This type of marriage is also lawful.

In some tribes the form of Gandharva marriage is a little different. Young boys and girls who are mature enough to get married are put in a huge house where they live together and choose their mates. It happens only within the tribe or between two or three neighboring tribes.

Swayamvara is one form of Gandharva marriage. Swayamvara means self-selection. The bride either goes around the circle of men invited for that purpose to select a mate, or she takes the man who wins a contest of some kind she or her parents choose.

8. *Paisaca.* This is the lowest type of marriage. The bride is taken away by fraud, or kidnapped by intoxicating her, and she is forcibly convinced to marry. This type of marriage is against the law and the society doesn't accept it.

Among the lower four forms of marriage, Rakshasas, Asura, and Gandharva marriages are in practice in different parts of the country. The first four forms were for Brahmins (scholarly class). The Rakshasas method was for Kshatriyas (warrior class). The Asura method was for Vaishya (business class) and Sudras (serving class). Gandharva method was accepted by all the castes except the Brahmins. But in the far past Brahmins also sometimes used the Gandharva method for marriage.

In the *Rig Veda* and *Atharva Veda* there is no mention of child marriage, but until recently people made a custom to get small boys and girls married. Probably this custom was started when India was being invaded by foreigners from time to time. Getting their children married was a way to make their friendship strong to face the foreigners attached together.

In the *Rig Veda* and *Atharva Veda,* marriage is considered to be a religious sacrament. A married woman has a very high status in society. She is considered equal to the man and takes part in the religious rites with her husband.

In the family a wife takes full responsibility for the household duties and she is considered as a guardian of all the members of the new family. Wives have higher rank in the house than the daughters (married, unmarried, or widows).

A wife is supposed to obey her husband as long as he lives, and after his death she should always respect his memory. A husband is supposed to support his wife because he accepts a wife as a gift from God. He should not think that he married her by his own will. In this way wife and husband surrender to each other and show their affection by doing their household duties thoroughly, by treating each other with love, by not committing adultery, by managing the household expenses within their earnings, by respect and faith to each other.

The marriage ceremonies have been changed much. Several rituals are forgotten and several new rituals are added. But still the main parts of the marriage rituals are observed according to the Vedas.

Marriage Rituals according to the Vedas

Marriage rituals in the *Rig Veda* and *Atharva Veda* are basically the same in spite of small differences, but the ceremony in the *Rig Veda* is much simpler.

1. *Negotiation.* The bridegroom's father goes to the bride's house, or sends a priest, for negotiation. They take with them fruits, flowers, and sweets to honor the family of the bride. The bride and bridegroom have their horoscopes cast. The bride is seen by the bridegroom's party. When the negotiations are concluded and the matter pleases both the parties, they touch a vessel of water into which have been put flowers, fried grain, fruits, and barley, which becomes a witness of their agreement.

2. *Selecting the Auspicious Day.* An auspicious day is chosen by an astrologer according to their horoscopes for the marriage, which is usually during the increasing phase of the moon and during the northern course of the sun. But one can also marry during the southern course of the sun.

3. *Ritual Bath.* The wedding is celebrated at the bride's father's house. The bridegroom and his relatives go there with their priest. At the beginning of the wedding the bride takes a purificatory bath. The basic idea is to wash away all dangerous influences on the bride. This bath is celebrated in different ways in different sects, castes, or tribes. Mostly they use yogurt and turmeric powder mixed to take the bath. Turmeric is a disinfectant and smoothes out the skin. This ritual is in the *Atharva Veda* and not mentioned in the *Rig Veda.*

4. *Clothing.* After the bath the bridegroom presents the bride with a new garment.

5. *Taking the Hands of the Bride.* The bridegroom takes the hands of the bride. Then blessings are given to the bride.

6. *Walking around the Fire.* The ceremony is performed in front of a sacred fire. The bride walks around the fire. In the *Atharva Veda* there is no mention of it. It could be a symbol of making the fire witness for the marriage. In *Griha Sutra* this ritual is one of the most important parts of the ceremony.

7. *Stepping on the Stone.* The bridegroom holds the hand of the bride and makes her step on a stone. The stone is a symbol of firmness and strength. This ritual is not mentioned in the *Rig Veda.*

8. *Removing the Evil Spirits.* Sacred verses are chanted to remove the evil spirits.

9. *Scattering Grains.* The bride scatters shriveled grains and prays for her husband's long life. This is one of the most important rituals of Hindu marriage. These fried grains are symbols of fruitfulness and prosperity.

10. *Bride's Leaving for Her New House.* When the bride leaves for her husband's house, as soon as the bridal procession starts, prayers are sung to make the journey successful.

11. *Sitting on the Hide.* The bride is made to sit over the hide of a bull. The hide should be from a red bull. The red color is a symbol of active nature and sitting on the hide is a symbol of fertility. This is mentioned as one of the important rituals in the *Atharva Veda,* but not mentioned in the *Rig Veda.*

12. *Consummation.* Sacred verses are chanted when the bride ascends the nuptial bed.

The rituals prescribed by the *Griha Sutras* are more complicated. Those rituals are arranged by the priests who were the authority in rites and rituals. They kept the Vedic structure of marriage intact and added things which they felt important. So the rituals of the *Griha Sutras* are most common everywhere in India, with a few variations in the different parts of India.

The marriage ceremonies prescribed by the *Griha Sutras* can be divided into two sections: magical and symbolical. Some rituals are done only to prevent the evil influences and have nothing to do with the marriage.

In the Vedas there is no mention of divorce. The marriage is considered a life-long agreement. But in *Kautalya Artha Shastra,* divorce is mentioned quite clearly:

The husband or wife cannot dissolve the marriage without each other's consent. They have to obtain divorce from mutual enmity. If the husband wants a divorce and gives full reasons for it, then he can get a divorce after returning everything which was given for the wife at the time of the marriage. If the wife wants a divorce and produces reasons for it, then she shall give up her claim to her property. But marriages of the first four kinds—Brahma, Daiva, Arsa, and Prajapatya—cannot be dissolved.

THE WEDDING CEREMONY ACCORDING TO SIKH TRADITION

A Sikh wedding is performed in the presence of the *Siri Guru Granth Sahib,* the "Living Guru of the Sikhs." The *Guru* is in the form of a book which is the compilation of songs of God from many major religions, including the ten Sikh gurus. What makes *Siri Guru Granth* a living guru is that when sung, the rhythm, sound, and ragas (musical scales) all combine to touch the higher consciousness of the person.

The couple bows before *Siri Guru Granth,* symbolizing that they are bowing before their higher consciousness. They then take their position sitting cross-legged facing the *Siri Guru Granth.* They meditate while the musicians begin to sing devotional shabds (songs).

The couple stands for the daily prayer (the ardas) of the Sikhs, which asks for guidance. Then a passage is read from the *Guru* which is to be a guiding light during their whole marriage. At this point the couple is ready to take the vows contained in the four nuptial rounds of the ceremony. The first vow is read by the priest. Along with each vow, the priest interprets in a practical sense what is required of the couple, what are their duties as a married couple, and warns them that they are making a life-long commitment.

The couple rises, and proceeds to walk around the *Guru*—the woman following the man, both holding onto a shawl, symbolizing their unity—while the magnificent vibrations of the music of the *Guru* absorbs them in their higher selves. When they return to their spots, they bring their foreheads to the ground to show that they have understood the vow. As they raise their heads, they indicate readiness to hear the second vow.

This same procedure is followed with the second, third, and fourth rounds. With their heads bowed for the fourth and final vow, the priest reminds them that this is it—they are committing themselves before God and *Guru*. If there is any doubt, they should not bring their heads up, and the marriage will not be consecrated.

If the man and woman raise their heads, the music starts again, and family and friends shower them with cut flowers, money, and any other gifts.

A final ardas, this time as a prayer of thanks, is given; then the blessed prasad (holy food which has been absorbing the vibrations of the ceremony) is given from the hands of the couple to each member of the congregation.

> Wahe Guru ji ka khalsa
> Wahe Guru ji ki fateh
>
> (The pure ones belong to God
> All victory goes to God)

INTERPRETATION OF THE SIKH WEDDING SONG (THE SIKH MARRIAGE VOWS)
BY GURU RAJ SINGH AND GURU RAJ KAUR

Our teacher, Yogi Bhajan, says, "The vows of the Sikh wedding are really four separate vows. You have to take them one at a time. If you understand, then catch each other's hand, and we'll go through with it, but if at any time you want to back out, then please do. Don't spoil your life and the life of your children and the life of all the people around you for the next fifty or sixty years because you feel you have to go through with it because your mother-in-law has spent all this money on the wedding."

He has often said at ceremonies, "See this hand you are holding. Let that hand be chopped off, or your head be chopped off, but do not let go of that hand." The commitment must be on this level because there are going to be a thousand things which will make you want to back out and separate. But it is the working out of the hassles, the surrendering and the sacrificing, one to the other, which creates strength and results in real love.

Not indulging in our emotional hang-ups is the real sacrifice. Sacrifice is not climbing up on a cross. It would be easy to be crucified, compared to the sacrifice of washing a dish when you don't feel like it. All of those little things that are in front of us all the time are the sacrifices which have real meaning. Those other big sacrifices are done for the sake of history.

We didn't know each other at all when we were married. We had just met three days before. We made a vow just the day before the wedding. We looked at each other and said, "Let's just make one promise: that we'll never walk away from each other angry or in the midst of an argument; we'll never say 'Ah, to hell with you' and walk away." That has proved to be a real sacrifice.

The First Vow

Proceeding forth into the first nuptial round, the Lord presents before you His instructions for the daily duties of marital life. Rather than the Vedas or Brahma, you are to recite the hymns of the Guru and be constant in the performance of your duty. Thus the errors of the past shall be washed away. Be confirmed in righteousness and repeat the Lord's name. The practice of the Name has been urged in the Simriks as well. Reflect upon the true Guru who is ever perfect, and all your sins and errors will leave you. By the greatest good fortune, the mind is filled with bliss, and thoughts of the Lord are soothing to the mind. Slave Narak proclaims that in this first round the marriage ceremony has begun.

This vow is very devotional. It is a vow to live in righteousness. This is done in several ways. This first is that the couple should regard themselves as the cornerstone of society, of God's kingdom on earth. A couple should see themselves as being the elemental economic and social unit of society, and should be self-sufficient unto each other as a social unit.

From that marriage bond will come the children, which are the future of the whole society. If the parents have that feeling of self-sufficiency and of contributing to society, then, of course, the children will grow up with that sense of responsibility and the sense of knowing that if anything is going to happen, it is going to be through them and through other human beings.

Secondly, it is your duty to share your earnings with the rest of society. Traditionally, this meant a tithe or one-tenth of your earnings. This can also be interpreted to mean that everyone must return to humanity, thereby to God, one-tenth of the energy he or she is putting out.

Thirdly, a true Sikh's work should be useful, gainful, and not involve the exploitation of others. Likewise, a husband and wife should not exploit each other. They should see themselves as being equals, although their energies may be different.

The Second Vow

Comes the second nuptial round, and the Lord has made ye to meet the true Guru. With your heart bound by the fear of the fearless God, all sense of pride has been washed from the mind. Knowing the fear of God and singing His praises, behold His presence before you. God, the Lord Master, is the Soul of the Creation. He pervades everywhere and fills all places with His Being. Know, then, that there is one God, within us and without, and the songs of His rejoicing are heard in the company of His servants. Navak proclaims that in this second nuptial round the Divine Music is heard.

This is the vow of truth. It is simple and straightforward. It means "I don't lie to you on any level or in any way, and you don't lie to me." It doesn't mean that we have to continually bare our souls to each other. It just means that we have a continual, simple understanding of truth, that we trust each other, that we tell each other the way it is and don't conceal or create illusions. This vow, like the first, is a cornerstone of a clear consciousness and a clear relationship.

We Sikhs say "Sat Nam": "God is Truth." That is the "fearless God" referred to in the vow. "Fear" is wrong terminology; it really means respect. When you have "respect" for that awesome awesomeness which surrounds us, then you understand that the only way to get even a little bit of a handle on it is through "Sat Nam," practicing fearless facing of the Truth in every way, large and small.

Not lying to one another means that we can trust each other so fully and completely that it is possible for us to expose our weakness to each other without being judged, and without having to depend on the other's strength for security. We relate to our own sense of truth and our own relationship with God for security. Therefore, it is possible to accept the weaknesses in each other because we just keep seeing the Truth in each other which is our highest potential, our true nature.

A marriage should not be a marriage of egos, defined in terms of "my strengths and your weaknesses." Marriage should be a marriage of soul, meaning "I am married to God and you are married to God." In a marriage, each of us, on an ego level, is very different. We come into conflict and are forced to transcend that and relate to our higher selves. This is a blessing.

The Third Vow

In the third round, the praises of the Lord fill my mind. By the greatest good fortune, you have come to meet the Lord God and the Company of the Holy. Singing His praises and speaking the Divine Word, the Immaculate Lord has been found. It is by great good fortune that the pious attain to the Lord, and tell that story which can never be told. The music of God resounds within, and we contemplate the Lord God, for we have been blessed with a great destiny written upon our foreheads. Slave

Navak proclaims that in this third round the love of God has been awakened in the heart.

This is the vow of love. It follows from the vow of Truth and elaborates on it. Once again it is saying "Do not regard your partner as an object of love." "God is the sole object of love." In loving another person you are loving *through* that person not *at* that person. Yogiji stresses that a love relationship between two people cannot be a business contract—"I love you and I will give you this if you will in return give me that." The love should be like that of a mother who gives to her child without reservation and without expectations of reward or return. Actually, love has nothing to do with anyone but *you;* it doesn't start or stop, and cannot be changed or tainted by anything. "Love is an *experience* of selflessness within one's self."

The Fourth Vow

In the fourth round, the mind grasps the knowledge of the Divine, and God is realized within. By the Guru's Grace, we have reached the Lord with ease. Our bodies and our souls are filled with the tender delight of the Beloved. I am a sacrifice unto my Lord. God seems sweet to me and I have become pleasing to my Master. He fills my thoughts all night and day. I have attained the object of my heart's desire, my Lord. By praising His Name, I have gained the highest praise. The Lord Himself becomes One with His holy bride. The heart of the bride blooms and flowers with His holy Name. Slave Navak proclaims that in the fourth round we have found the Eternal Lord.

This is the vow of devotion. We reiterate the fact that the whole object of the marriage is to reach God. There are endless ways in which this takes place—in standing together, in serving together, in creating children together, and so on. All these things create God around you.

We also solidify our commitment to do sadhana together. We commit ourselves to get up before the rise of the sun for the rest of our lives, to thank God each day for what came before and for what is about to come, to realize that everything comes from Infinity and everything returns to that same Infinite Source. It is a commitment to continually purify ourselves, to clean out negativity and tension in the relationship so that we may become more compassionate and loving.

THE ZEN-BUDDHIST WEDDING CEREMONY
TRANSLATED FROM THE TRADITIONAL SOTO ZEN CEREMONY BY KENNETT ROSHI

(First procession, doan, celebrant, and jiisha; second procession, thurifer and bride. Quatz, three gongs for incense offering, and Scripture of Great Wisdom, offertory and Scripture verse. Celebrant:-)

We worship the Great Lord Shakyamuni Buddha, Koso Joyo Daishi, Taiso Josai Daishi and all the Three Treasures in all directions and in the three periods of time. Here there are an excellent man and woman who are marrying each other since their excellent relationship has been consummated and prepared from ages past. Because of this they now stand before the Lord and beg to attain his benefits. They are praying deeply to the Three Treasures and to all the Buddhas for their protection. I am going to permit them to live together in pleasure and in pain, in happiness and unhappiness until a ripe old age and to endeavour to offer the merits thereof to all creatures. I pray that the True Light of the Lord may shine on their excellent minds thus purifying both their body and their mind.

(Bride and groom stand together. The celebrant turns round, takes the asperge and asperges them, saying:-)

Say together after me:-

> I take my refuge in the Buddha;
> That I may realize the True Way and the
>   Highest Mind I wish to help all
>   living things.
> I take my refuge in the Dharma;
> I wish to help all living things in order
>   to enter the Store of the Scriptures
>   so that I may make the wisdom of
>   this my family as wide as the ocean.
> I take my refuge in the Sangha;
> I wish to help all living things so that
>   they and my family shall possess an
>   immaculate and peaceful heart.

(Celebrant:-)

Do you take this woman to be your lawful wedded wife?

(Groom:-)
   I do.
(Celebrant:-)
   Do you take this man to be your lawful wedded husband?
(Bride:-)
   I do.
(The celebrant takes the rings and censes them. Giving one to the groom, he says:-)
   Repeat after me:-

> With this ring I thee wed;
> With my body I thee worship;
> With all my worldly goods I thee endow;
> And thereto I plight thee my troth.*

(The celebrant gives the other ring to the bride who puts it on the groom's finger in the same way as he put the first one on hers, repeating the above also. The celebrant holds the wedding candle and both the bride and groom light it with the candles they are holding; they then blow out their individual candles and give them to their attendants. The celebrant takes his rosary and binds the right hands of the bride and groom together, places the Nyoi on top of the bound hands and says:-)

By the authority vested in me, I pronounce that you are man and wife together. Thus joined together, this bond can never be sundered.

(The jiisha takes the marriage contract and certificate and hands the former to the celebrant who censes it and hands it to the bride and groom who read it together:-)

We are now being given the Light of the Lord which is full of grace so that we have been able to marry each other. From this time we are going to be converted deeply to the Three Treasures and make both our bodies and minds pure so that we may make no mistakes in human morals. We are going to help each other and make each of us successful in our own way. We offer the merits of all we do for the welfare of all mankind.

(Both bride and groom sign the marriage contract and the certificate together with the witnesses. Celebrant:-)

Let us live in the world as if in the sky just as the lotus blossom is not wetted by the water that surrounds it. Let our minds be immaculate and beyond all uncleanness. Let us bow our heads to the Highest Lord.

*This section was taken from the old Church of England ceremony.

> I vow to save others endlessly.
> I vow to cease from desire for eternity.
> I vow to study the Dharma for ever.
> I vow to perfect Buddhism in all lives
>   and in all worlds.

(The doan, celebrant, and jiisha proceed out of the hall followed by the bride and groom.)

Setting up the Room

There should be two vases of flowers, i.e., two baby pine trees or two pine branches, cakes, and fruit on the altar. There should be an asperge bowl, rosary, and the necessary legal papers upon the high altar; the wooden blocks, incense bowl, incense box, and writing materials are placed on the side altar. The celebrant's assistant carries the celebrant's ceremony book. The relatives of the groom are seated on the right side of the room, and those of the bride on the left.

Explanation of Terms Used in the Ceremony

1. *Doan*—the presenter or person leading the scriptures
2. *Celebrant*—the Zen priest officiating at the ceremony
3. *Jiisha*—the celebrant's attendant
4. *Thurifer*—the person carrying the incense holder
5. *Quatz*—musical procession (bell, drum, and cymbals)
6. *Shakyamuni Buddha*—the historical Buddha living during the sixth century, B.C.
7. *Koso Joyo Daishi (Dogen)*—the Zen Master who brought Soto Zen from China to Japan in the thirteenth century
8. *Taiso Josai Daishi (Keizan)*—the Zen Master who spread Soto Zen throughout Japan in the fourteenth century
9. *Three Treasures*—the Buddha, dharma, sangha (see below)
10. *Buddha*—literally, the "Enlightened One"; refers to one's own true nature
11. *Dharma*—teaching, truth, law
12. *Sangha*—community of Buddhist trainees
13. *Asperge*—small branch used to sprinkle water as an act of purification
14. *Nyoi*—small staff carried by the celebrant

MEDITATION TO INTEGRATE THE
SANCTITY OF MARRIAGE

Place four candles in a rectangle.

1. Sit together quietly, the husband on the right of the wife. After a few minutes together, light the first candle, which symbolizes "one soul in two bodies." Contemplate the bond of your complementary natures, and concentrating in your hearts, feel love for your mutual source.
2. After a few minutes light the second candle, which symbolizes your life together as husband and wife, which is your yoga. Feel in your hearts love and understanding of your eternal unity, and contemplate the sacrifice of personal desires that living this unity will mean.
3. Light the third candle, which symbolizes your future children. Feel love within your hearts for your children, praying that you as parents will be able to pass virtue on to them, through the example of your love and understanding.
4. Now light the fourth candle, which symbolizes the family of mankind. Feel in your hearts the connection of your family to all the families of humanity.

Praise God.

INDIVIDUAL CONTRIBUTORS

MEHER BABA was a well-known Indian saint who died in 1969.

JOHN G. BENNETT was a renowned author, teacher of the Gurdjieff School, and acknowledged authority on Sufism.

REB SCHLOMO CARLEBACH, known as "the singing rabbi," is a Jewish mystic who shares stories, teachings, and songs with people wherever he goes.

BABA HARI DASS became famous in the West as the silent yogi in *Be Here Now*. He is a master of Ashtanga Yoga (eight-limbed yoga) and teaches extensively in the United States and Canada. He is the author of *The Yellow Book* and *Silence Speaks*.

RAM DASS is a well-known New Age teacher and author.

ROY EUGENE DAVIS, a direct disciple of Paramahansa Yogananda, is a well-known author and teacher of Kriya Yoga.

GAYATRI DEVI is a member of the Temple of Cosmic Religion, Vanderbilt, Michigan.

DHARMASARA SATSANG is a group of devotees of Baba Hari Dass, who live in Vancouver, British Columbia. Ravi Dass and Aparna, editors of this volume, are members of Dharmasara.

RESHAD FIELD is a sheikh of the Mevlevi Dervishes, and head of the Mevlevi Dervish Order in the West. He is the author of *The Last Barrier*.

SUDARSHAN FILKOW is a practicing lawyer and legal counselor to the New Age community in Vancouver, Canada.

STEPHEN GASKIN is the leader of the largest spiritual community in North America, The Farm, and is the author of numerous books, including *Monday Night Class* and *This Season's People*. His wife, INA MAY GASKIN, is a teacher of natural childbirth methods, and is the author of *Spiritual Midwifery*.

MURSHID MOINEDDIN JABLONSKI is one of the senior Sufi Order teachers in the San Francisco Bay area.

HAZRAT INAYAT KHAN was the founder of the modern Sufi Order in the West.

PIR VILAYAT INAYAT KHAN is the son of the late Hazrat Inayat Khan, and is the present head of the Sufi Order in the West. He is the author of *Toward the One*.

TOM KOPKA is a student of Baba Hari Dass and a practicing householder yogi.

SWAMI KRIYANANDA is a direct disciple of Paramahansa Yogananda. A teacher of yoga and author of *The Path—Autobiography of a Western Yogi,* he is the founder/director of Ananda Cooperative Village, Nevada City, California.

MURSHID SAMUEL LEWIS was a Western Sufi master who popularized Sufi dancing. He is well known for having made the hidden concepts of several major religions available for Western understanding.

GEORGE MCCLURE is a college professor at Washington State and is a practicing householder yogi.

MAHESH NAUD is a founding member of Dharmasara Satsang.

DIANA NISSON is an author of children's books and the mother of two.

PHILIP AND ELLEN are founding members of The Farm, Stephen Gaskin's community in Tennessee.

HILDA PICKERING is a gentle old lady and a student of the teachings of Jesus Christ.

REB ZALMAN SCHACHTER is a Hassidic rabbi and Sufi sheikh. He is the author of *Fragments of a Future Scroll.* He is joined in the present work by his wife ELANA.

PANDIT GIAN CHANDRA SHASTRI is the temple priest at the Vishwa Hindu Parishad, in Vancouver, British Columbia.

RABBI DANIEL SIEGEL is a practicing rabbi in Vancouver, British Columbia.

KIRPAL SINGH was a master of Surad Shabd Yoga, and the author of many books on spirituality.

GURU RAJ SINGH and his wife GURU RAJ KAUR are co-directors of the 3HO Foundation in Vancouver, British Columbia. They are founding members of the World Symposium on Humanity.

PATRICIA SUN is a New Age spiritual teacher from Berkeley, California.

BARRY AND JOYCE VISSELL are "spiritual" psychotherapists, who work with couples from various New Age spiritual groups in the Santa Cruz, California, area.

MORDECHAI and HANA WOSK have lived and studied Judaism in Jerusalem.